P9-ELP-560

Scatter My Ashes Over Havana

Scatter My Ashes Over Havana

A memoir by
Olga Karman

Pureplay Press
Los Angeles

First Edition

Copyright © 2006 Olga Karman

All rights reserved under International and Pan-American Copyright Conventions.

No part of this book may be reproduced or transmitted in any form or by any means, electronic or mechanical, including photocopying and recording, or by any information storage or retrieval system without the prior written permission of the copyright owner unless such copying is expressly permitted by federal copyright law.

Please direct all correspondence to: editor@pureplaypress.com / Pureplay Press, 11353 Missouri Ave., Los Angeles, CA 90025.

Cataloguing-in-Publication Data
Karman, Olga.
   Scatter My Ashes Over Havana : a memoir / by Olga Karman. — 1. Ed.
         p. cm.
ISBN (10-digit) 0-9765096-4-4 (13-digit) 978-0-9765096-4-6
1. Karman, Olga. 2. Cuba — History — Revolution, 1959- — Personal narratives. 3. United States — History — Nineteen sixties — Personal narratives. 4. Buffalo (N.Y.) — Biography. 5. Karman, Olga — Childhood and youth. 6. Havana (Cuba) — Biography. 7. Immigrants — United States — Biography. 8. Hispanic Americans — Social life and customs — Biography. 9. Connecticut College — Biography. 10. Harvard University — Biography. I. Title
973.046—dc22

Library of Congress Control Number: 2006903385

Author photo by Federico R. Justiniani

Additional photos from archives of the author and of Pureplay Press

Cover and book design by Wakeford Gong

Printed in the United States

Scatter My Ashes
Over Havana

PART I

Good Morning, Sadness

*PLEASE PLEASE BE THERE, **Aleesofee**, please be there.* I rushed past the long queue in front of the American Embassy, wanting to be invisible; I kept my eyes forward, trying not to let on that I was about to climb the grass-covered rise and make a dash for the side door, for Alice Sophie. "All you have to do," our school principal had said, "is knock on the side door at ten. Ten on the dot. She'll be there." I didn't quite believe it.

A blur of freckles and white-blond hair, Alice Sophie yanked me inside. *"¡Corre!* Run!" Off we flew, just as we had on the school basketball court, dodging embassy workers who were running with stacks of folders in their arms and calling out to each other in English, "Take the back stairs! Get rid of those! The afternoon flight! Diplomatic pouch!"

Why are they hurrying? What's the rush? Then it hit me as hard as newsprint: *Cuba se hunde. Cuba is sinking.* But what about our nickname, "the island made of cork"? Wasn't that supposed to be a kind of talisman?

Alice Sophie and I barged into an office. A man in a seer-sucker suit looked up, grabbed my passport, stamped it, and back we flew to the side door. *!Gracias, Aleesofee, adiós!* A metal door slammed shut, and out in the heat I felt the phrase I'd learned in history class: *Alea iacta est*—the die is cast. And so it was.

In a daze, I couldn't think which way to turn—even though the seawall on Paseo del Malecón, where I'd often sat after school with Alejandro, Elvira and Evelio, was in plain sight. My teenage turf had become a foreign country. I moved tentatively; I was a stranger, a fugitive. An illustration from my childhood catechism flashed before me: Adam and Eve, cast out of paradise, walking away from Eden in shame as the angel stood guard with his flam-ing sword. My damp fingers were stuck together; my perspiration had melted the glue under the passport's gauze cover. Where was my car? Where was I?

Not thinking, I walked right into the queue of men and women baking on the treeless sidewalk in front of the embassy. By mis-take, I had intruded on their eerie silence—a woeful emptiness in a place where once everyone had thrived on banter and wordplay. A malignant spell had befallen us. A witty and gregarious people had been cowed into dumbness; our blue-and-gold city had gone mute and solemn. It was, I supposed, what Budapest or Prague must be like. Under the harsh daylight, some in the queue were holding up the official daily paper *Revolución* to shade their heads. The irony made me gasp: people blocking the sun with the very words that had twisted their lives and mine.

I walked on through the maelstrom of a fleeing population. Family, friends and neighbors who had made up my place in the world were all blowing away. I felt blindsided by a desolation that had overcome me after I'd given a strong *yes* to my American boyfriend's marriage proposal. I had said *yes* to a country where the ocean wouldn't hem me in; where I might live far from the perfect rows of royal palms that reminded me an island could be a prison. I had said *yes* to my American dreams because, having just turned twenty, I wanted more. And now that I was about to get it, *more* felt many sizes too big. As we used to say in Havana, I'd gotten myself into an eleven-yard shirt.

A slow-moving car pulled up right next to me. I could feel its heat. The driver stuck out his head and hollered: *"¡GUSANA! ¡VETE PA'L CARAJO!* Hey, you worm! To hell with you!" *Worms:* That's what Fidel Castro called us, the ones who were leaving his socialist paradise. I pretended to ignore the driver, but I couldn't breathe. My hands were wet and shaking.

On the drive home, I forced myself to stop feeling. I had to survive what was coming. Upstairs in my room, I started to make a pile of the things I must leave behind. I chucked in my diary without reading a single word; my autograph book; the manila envelope with the 8x10 graduation photo of Evelio next to me in his white tux; my Ruston Academy yearbooks; the English compositions that Mrs. Thurman had praised. I was making a sacrificial mound in order to transform those beloved objects into remains I could forget: the Duncan yo-yo badge I'd won at a Teatro Miramar contest; my 50-meter swim-meet medal; a baseball autographed by Minnie Miñoso; my cowgirl riding boots; a studio glossy of Mario Lanza; a framed 8x10 of Fidel Castro mid-speech, with his index finger up in the air; my first Communion missal; *Black Beauty, The Old Man and the Sea, Little Women, Introduction to Psychiatry,* José Martí's *Versos sencillos, Platero y yo* and of course Françoise Sagan's *Bonjour tristesse.*

Father rolled down the windows to cool off the station wagon. I waited on the curb next to my three mouse-colored cardboard suitcases, the only ones Mother and I were able to find because, with so many people leaving Havana, the stores were sold out. On the morning of my first Communion, I'd stood under this very same orange mimosa, waiting for the car to cool down. I was eight years old, in a long white organza gown and ballooning veil; my drawstring handbag was embroidered with a chalice and a cross; I carried grandmother's mother-of-pearl missal. Our calico,

Cusita, rubbed against my gown, and when I bent down to pet her I found mud on my white patent-leather shoes. Dirty shoes for a holy day; I was going to my first Communion unclean. And now, deserting Cuba, I had a new stain.

Celita and Gloria came to say goodbye; kiss, kiss. We were three lanky young girls barely out of their teens. In dark suit and heels, I was the one out of character. Where was the uniform—the pedal pushers and sandals? I was masquerading as a grown-up.

Father loaded the suitcases, and the car began to pull away from my world. I squinted to make all of it a blur: Señor Mesa's loud parrots and fire-colored macaws, Miramar Grocery, Cervera's *farmacia*, Pepe Cancio's *bodega*, one long blur. And then it was gone, and I knew I was not coming back.

In minutes we were pulling up to Mama Angélica's house in Vedado. There she stood waiting on her porch, in widow's black although Papa Karman had been dead five years. I made room for grandmother in the back seat, took her hand. A wordless dread spilled over me; Mama had to sense it. She began a series of gay little comments, more like chirps. She opened her sandalwood fan and fluttered it to send a little draft my way. When she closed it, the sound was of someone shuffling a deck of cards. *How does she do that? I should've learned. Now there's no time left.*

Now near Havana Harbor, I could smell the ocean and see the dock; my big ship, the *Guadalupe,* was looming over the Avenida del Puerto cafés. *One big wave,* I thought, *and that ship would rise up and kill everyone in those cafés.*

Before I knew what was happening, I was all by myself inside the passenger area, and a hard-faced, muscle-bound militia woman in olive green uniform and black lace-up boots was ordering: "Come with me!" Swimming before my eyes was a sea of olive-green, the Revolution's regulation color. Once upon a time, right after the Revolution's triumph, olive green had stood for the victory of good over evil; and I had believed in it—oh, how I had believed—with all my heart.

"Take off your clothes!" She had stepped inside the cubicle

with me. I heard her, but the simple words were unintelligible. "I repeat. Take everything off. *Todo.*" I took off the black "travel suit" that Mother had made for me out of Papa Karman's tuxedo and, sensing the woman's impatience, left it in a heap on the dusty floor. "Separate your legs. Jump up and down with your arms raised over your head." I was naked, jumping and choking with rage. From the next cubicle came a scuffle, then wailing; a passenger had been caught trying to smuggle jewels inside her "beehive" hairdo. *What if Mother and Father have hidden something inside my luggage? But wait—how can I think such thoughts? This is what the Revolution has done. We don't even trust our own parents.*

"Get dressed!" The *miliciana* led me past a glass wall. Mother, Father and Mama Angélica were on the other side. *I can't breathe. How can I undo all this?* We wouldn't be able to hear each other's voices again, or touch. When I slid my index fingers down my cheeks, they looked away. *How can I make this stop? Do I dare to? Do I want to?* From the mast of a Soviet tanker at anchor next to the *Guadalupe,* a big hammer-and-sickle flag was waving impudently. Red flag, red Cuba. *I can't stay.*

Hey, militia lady! Your uniform is the last olive green I'll ever have to obey!

If only it were so easy.

❊ ❊ ❊

Two years before, the Olive-Green Revolution had filled us all with hope. In the few seconds it took me to follow the *miliciana* from the cubicle to the boarding area, those two years of turbulence engulfed me all over again.

The glory days had begun before sunrise of New Year's Day 1959 with an anonymous phone call to our home in Miramar, and a voice declaring: *"¡El hombre se fue!* The man has gone!" *The man,* corrupt and cruel dictator Fulgencio Batista, had been in power since his 1952 coup. Neighbors were on their porches in pajamas. They stood on sidewalks and waved at each other with upturned palms as if to ask: *What happened?* The first newscasts were noncommittal: "Movement has been observed on the road to the Columbia army base. Planes have been seen taking off from the Columbia airstrip." But as the hours passed, more and more frequently came the cry, *"¡Viva Cuba! ¡Viva la Revolución!"* When we heard the first notes of the Cuban national anthem, Papi stood up to sing and so did Mami, while my twin brother Roberto, copying Father, placed his right hand over his heart.

Pandemonium had broken out. Radios blared military marches; cars sped along Quinta Avenida beeping horns and flying the red-and-black flags of the victorious 26th of July Movement; people fired shots into the air and men wielding sledgehammers knocked down parking meters.

A week later, Fidel's motorcade, having crossed the island all the way from Oriente province, arrived in Havana. Carrying a bouquet of garden flowers wrapped in newspaper, I went to welcome my hero and waited along Calzada de Columbia avenue, where those with portable radios kept the rest of us posted: *Fidel is this close, only a few more minutes.* Then, in the distance, an olive-green cloud took shape; an army of beards and longhairs came toward us, a number of them riding in open trucks and jeeps, and lots of other men shuffling along, most of them strangely silent, not keeping formation because they were a *real people's army* and not a dictator's wind-up army. Fidel, a giant in olive-green fatigues, rode by on a tank, solemn. I was stunned, frozen in place. Long after he'd gone by, I was still holding his flowers.

Fidel's first Havana speech from Camp Columbia was heartstopping; a white dove settled on his shoulder and remained there oblivious to his emphatic gestures. That dove—what could it be but a sign of the Holy Spirit? Some thought it showed Fidel to be a favored son of African *santos.*

The next days and weeks were full of Fidel's speeches—five-, six-, seven-hour discourses that Mother, Father, my twin brother Roberto and I heard without making a sound or moving at all except when one of us had to sprint to the bathroom. We returned to the sofa half-zipped, whispering: "What did he say? What did I miss?" Fidel moved us so deeply at first that we often hid our tears from each other even though we were all sitting together on the same living-room sofa.

Barbudos, the bearded revolutionary soldiers, were instant celebrities. Spotting them became a new sport: "There was one on my bus!" "Run, there's one with a machine gun right on the corner!" We walked up to them and said *gracias;* children poked at their beards and fingered the rosaries around their necks. Some people said the rosaries had been "planted" to make us believe the Revolution wasn't communist. What cynics they were!

One night I watched a TV special about wounded *barbudos* convalescing at the military hospital. They were so wretched: napalm burns, arms in casts, bandaged stumps in place of legs. One after another told the reporter he wanted to return home to family and crops. Some looked into the camera and, wide-eyed, addressed their relatives: *"Cuca, how are you?"* The man paused, as if waiting for Cuca to answer. *"Cuca! Tell Joseíto I'm coming to help him out."* Pause. *"Arsenio, did you get the corn planted? Any rain?"*

And so I volunteered to work at the army hospital.

I set up a desk in the hospital patio and waited for the shy soldiers to approach me. Gradually they came out of their rooms, curious. I offered to help them with letters home. *Tell me what you want to say, and I'll write it and send it.* So they talked about what they'd done, and they said it was what anyone would have done for his country.

So far, so good; but then they had to tell me how to address their letters.

"The letter? Oh! Send it to *mi casa.*"

"Okay, what's the address?"

"Well, you see, *mi casa* is right there, outside Ceiba del Agua. You know, just a short walk away from the Instituto."

"*¿Mi casa?* It's the second *bohío* after you pass the Curve of the Singing Frog."

The men moved me to tears, which I had to hold back until the ride home. I drove reciting verses by José Martí:

> *Con los pobres de la Tierra*
> *quiero yo mi suerte echar;*
> *el arroyo de la sierra*
> *me complace más que el mar.*

> (With the poor of the Earth
> do I cast my destiny;
> the mountain's limpid stream
> is more pleasing than the sea.)

✻ ✻ ✻

Long before January 1959, I'd seen the poor of the earth up close. They were skinny, barefoot children, their bellies puffed up with tapeworms, living in remote places where huts dotted the countryside. On a morning five or six years earlier, when I was about twelve, I'd stopped at one of these *bohíos* or thatched-roof huts to ask for a drink of water.

"Get off that horse. Get out of that sun. Go on in. It's lunchtime," the man of the house commanded me as if I were his own child. He took hold of Sultán's reins and waited for me to dismount. His wife brought me a gourd full of water and invited me to sit on their dirt floor. I sat and cooled off while she boiled roots and three eggs at the wood stove. When the time came to eat she turned to me and smiled, covering her mouth so I wouldn't see her toothless gums. I ran my tongue over the expensive braces that Dr. Giquel had put on me the week before, and I hated my own good fortune. *Why did I get all the luck? What am I going to do about it? They're eating less today because I'm here. Look at that. Three eggs for four people!*

I wanted to hand them my horse, my cowgirl boots, the clothes I was wearing. I rode back to our farm on fire, wiping my tears with the back of my hand, the horse leading the way. *How does a girl change things? Someday when I grow up I'll come and save them. I promise.*

That moment was Cuba's gift to me, its everlasting mark. *With the poor of the earth do I cast my destiny.* Yes, when the Revolution came, I was ready.

* * *

On a morning in early 1959, an orderly presented himself at my hospital desk and asked me to follow him. His major, a *comandante* in Fidel's victorious Rebel Army, wanted to see me. The *comandante*, a thin, dark-skinned man in olive-green fatigues, crackled with tension as he went storming about his office, bumping into massive mahogany furniture that the old régime had left behind. Eventually he noticed me. Brushing away the orderlies who were trying to hand him papers to sign, he escorted them all out, closed the door and sat at his desk. Then he looked at me and blurted: "I can't read or write. Teach me."

I set to it right away. After half an hour, the *comandante* walked me to a globe of the world.

"*Maestra,*" he called me—*teacher,* although he was double my eighteen years—"show me. Where is Vienna?"

"That's Vienna—right there."

He rested his fingertip on that spot of the globe as if to feel the city. "*Maestra,* teach me to dance the waltz, just as they do in that film, *The Merry Widow.* When things quiet down, we'll take one of those MiG's on the runway, fly to Vienna and dance the waltz."

At home, while my family and I were having dinner, the *comandante*'s driver rang our doorbell and announced the officer. In walked my olive-green-uniformed student. He came right up to Father and spoke with respect but also with authority. "I request your permission to take my *maestra* and her mother to Vienna, the capital of Austria."

As the black Oldsmobile pulled away, arguments broke out. **No** to Vienna! **No** to the *comandante*'s lessons! I ran to my room, slamming doors as I went, but it was all theater. I was relieved. What would I have done with a grown man in Vienna? What did I know about Vienna, or about grown men?

*   *   *

The Revolution's glory days were fleeting. Fidel was shutting down newspapers, fanning hatred among social classes. It seemed he was even getting ready to close my university, Santo Tomás de Villanueva. Could anyone reason with Fidel? I thought I could. My classmates thought we could. Why not intercept him on the Guiteras Bridge, where he sometimes passed at day's end? Surely we would convince him.

We waited on the dark bridge, rehearsing our lines. *Don't close Villanueva! Let us study so we can contribute to the new Cuba after we graduate!*

An Oldsmobile's headlights appeared and we ran out onto the road, grabbing each other's hands to form a barricade. The driver slammed on the brakes. Before the Olds had come to a full stop, the passenger door flew open and out jumped Fidel. Celia Sánchez, his intimate *compañera*, was hissing orders at the driver.

"What's going on here?" Fidel demanded. His brusque tone scared me.

Once he realized he was in no danger, Fidel walked us to the guardrail and calmly began telling us about Abraham Lincoln and social justice. "All people were not created equal. They weren't, but we have to proceed as if they were. And those with the greatest needs have to be first."

Those with the greatest needs: that meant the woman in the *bohío* hiding her toothless gums, didn't it?

He asked us one by one what we were studying at Villanueva. As we spoke, he leaned his olive-green figure into each of us as if hearing confession. *He's eating out of our hands. He'll give us what we want.* As Fidel got back in the Olds, I slipped Celia Sánchez the note I'd prepared.

Dear Fidel,

You look tired on TV. My Uncle Miguel has a small farm just outside Alquízar. He'd like you to go there and rest. We won't bother you. My phone number is B-7427.

Your admirer,
Olga Karman

He hardly needed the invitation. Fidel's *barbudos* were already bivouacked at our farm. Tío Miguel, the day of his last visit, had found five men in olive green sitting on his rocking chairs. Uncle had also found a strange-looking rations tin on the ground. The label was in Cyrillic; these were Soviet rations.

Our twenty acres aren't ours anymore, Miguel had told us. Like any good Cuban, he'd tempered the news with a joke.

"What tree does the Revolution resemble?"

"It resembles the palm tree. That's what Fidel says: 'The Revolution is as green as the palms—*verde como las palmas.*' It's not red, not communist. Why? What tree do *you* think it resembles?"

"The guava tree."

"Why the guava?"

"Green on the outside, red on the inside."

* * *

As that Oldsmobile bore Fidel away, my schoolmates and I were frantically comparing notes. The realization came quickly. "You mean he didn't promise us anything?"

Fidel had left us empty-handed. Indeed, he'd done what he did best: he'd pulled us into his magnetic field, and our compass needles had gone haywire.

Clearly, our university was about to be closed. But I was not ready to give up on the Revolution. I waited to see how Fidel would explain what he was doing. I felt sure he would reconcile the facts into a higher truth. On a memorable Sunday afternoon, Fidel addressed a crowd of half a million people from a terrace of the Presidential Palace.

I was there. He talked to us about national elections. A bad idea, elections—or so he said. The enemies of the Revolution were pressing him for elections, but what they really wanted was to destabilize the country. We didn't need elections.

He worked the crowd into a frenzy, then bellowed: "I ask the people"—theatrical pause to let the crowd feel his power in the silence—"I ask *el pueblo*, does *el pueblo* want elections?"

El pueblo, half-a-million strong, yelled back: "Noooooo! Nooooooooo!" They were "voting" with handkerchiefs, leaflets, whatever they could get their hands on. And Fidel: "The people have voted. *El pueblo ha votado.*" Then came the rhythmic chanting: "Fi-DEL, Fi-DEL, Fi-DEL."

Adiós, revolutionary dreams. *Adiós*, whatever was left of my trust in Fidel. For the first time his voice had sounded hollow, and I listened no more. "Good morning, sadness," I repeated to myself on the way home from the enormous rally, borrowing the title of Françoise Sagan's novel *Bonjour tristesse*—a book that people termed "risqué."

But really, French risqué was child's play compared to a single man persuading those multitudes to give up their voices.

When I stopped listening to Fidel, I gained in personal freedom but I became an outcast in my own country. My spirit had gone into exile, and I could only follow.

Soledad

THE *GUADALUPE* BEGAN TO SHUDDER and back out of her mooring. To my left was Havana—part of my own silhouette. Right in front of me, Father, Mother and Mama Angélica were leaving the dock at a run, Father helping Mama Angélica.

Look at them rushing away! How little they must love me! What can I expect? I'm abandoning them.

But when the ship reached the mouth of the harbor, I could see three forlorn figures on the esplanade that we call La Punta, just across from the Morro Castle. There stood my loved ones, waiting for the *Guadalupe* to pass by, each waving a white handkerchief.

Mother! Father! Mama Angélica! Here I am! Over here, on the deck! How small you look, how frail, waving those handkerchiefs! I wish you wouldn't do that. Stop doing that!

I looked down at the ocean. Black and bossy, it seemed to be yelling up at me: *Jump!*

Glancing back to shore, I thought I saw a phantom of myself

standing with the three figures, waving back at me and seeming as forlorn as the others.

Which of these was I—the rootless one on the ship, or the heavy-hearted ghost on solid ground?

The figures turned to haze, and the coastline became a haze. My eyes began to well up until an urgent voice, barking in the loud wind, commanded me: *Don't cry. There's no one here who can hold you. You'll fall apart if you start crying. Get indoors.*

I turned my back on the wind and went inside; then strode to the bar and ordered a Johnnie Walker.

"Red or Black, *señorita?*" the bartender questioned.

How do I know? Just answer! Don't let life see you miss a beat, or it will swallow you whole.

"Black."

A man in starched whites—*no more olive green, thank God*—was toasting me. It was the ship's purser. He looked like Father—large brown eyes, thin nose—but spoke with a Castilian lisp. *"Buen viaje,"* he said, giving me a Spaniard's *bon voyage.* When I raised my glass to his, my hand quivered so badly that the ice cubes jingled against the sides of the glass. One sip, then another, and a quietness began to swell in me like tissue around a wound.

*   *   *

All I now owned was the trousseau contained in my cardboard suitcases. I fled back to the stateroom and buried my face inside the layers of vaporous nightgowns—peach, baby blue, white for the wedding night and a frightening, provocative black one with a tiny baby-blue bow.

I had shopped for these at El Encanto, the well-known Havana department store where Mother was director of personnel. For shopping companions, I had had my friends Elvira and Andrea, who came to the store with me a number of times. In the bridal salon, the three of us rummaged through *déshabillés* and *négligés*, then snatched up a quantity and marched into the fitting rooms. While I tried on the delicate things over my slip, Elvira and Andrea acted out wedding-night scenes, rolling their eyes, panting, shoving, belly-laughing, grabbing me and impersonating the groom in their fractured English: "*I lof you, I lof you.*"

The three of us, not quite women yet, were in love with love among the finery, trying in those hours to live as if the ground under us were steady—as if our existences weren't about to become unrecognizable. Those visits to El Encanto were our respite from the six-inch headlines in *Revolución* announcing the closure of one more "counterrevolutionary" newspaper, the seizure of one more "capitalist worm's" property, the proclamation of one more plan from Fidel Castro's bottomless pit, or the latest rumor of an impending *yanqui* invasion.

A gentle knock at the stateroom door broke my reverie. Before I could ask *who is it* the purser in starched whites had let himself in. He secured the lock, stretched out on my bed, unfastened his belt, took me by the hand and said, "lie down," pulling me to him.

The ship's engines were loud. Even if my throat could open, who would hear me scream? But then, from a strength I hadn't known, I took heart and counterattacked.

I held his hand and started telling him stories. *Did you read what Herbert Matthews wrote about Fidel in* The New York Times? *My real hero is Camilo Cienfuegos. I had a crush on Camilo, to tell you the truth, but he died in a plane crash. Some say Fidel had him killed. Maybe he did. I'm not sure.*

The purser half-listened, tugging at my clothes. I demurred, holding his hand firmly under mine. *Did you hear about Batista's torture chambers?* I asked him tenderly. *Straight pliers for pulling out fingernails, a metal scoop for eyeballs and another one for crushing testicles. I actually saw all this on display at the Havana Riviera Hotel. You're from Spain, aren't you? Do they torture men in Spain? Did you hear about Fidel's war-crimes trials? I translated at those trials for an American journalist. At dinner he didn't eat shrimp. He said he wouldn't eat creatures that crawled. Do you think that's a religious thing, or could it be allergies? I have a horse named Sultán. Do you like horses? I prefer dapple-grays. I sail too. One day I saw a shark's fin appear and disappear next to my sailboat. It looked like this. Watch. A manta ray too, but on a different day. It was so wide that I could see one wing tip from the starboard side and the other from the port side. And ... and ... and ...*

A phrase at a time, I was extricating myself.

"Forget New York!" he finally blurted out. "How can an American make you happy? Come to Spain with me." He wanted to put me up in his flat in Seville. He said his mother would take care of me while he was at sea. *Am I that young?* I wondered to myself. I asked him his mother's name. It was Soledad.

"*Soledad, Soledad,*" I repeated. "What a beautiful name. *Soledad, Soledad,*" I called out again and again, "*Soledad, Soledad.*"

He got up, stumbled into the bathroom and heaved, thrashing between groans. I'd never heard anything like that. The violence was new to me. I could see him leaning against the bathroom wall, trying to rest. He came toward me and made a statement an inch from my face: "No woman has ever given me so much or so little." Then he stumbled out of the cabin.

I had no idea what he meant, but as soon as he left I shoved my three suitcases on the floor end to end, barricading the door. Night became dawn. In the early morning light he was on the deck outside my room, his knuckles rapping on the porthole. I drew the curtain shut, making myself small in bed, hugging myself. I had not undressed but my hands felt cold. My fingernails had dug ridges into my arms.

Time passed, I don't know how much. I was still confused and drowsy when I heard seagulls and noticed that the ship's engines had gone silent. Drawing the curtains open, I looked out a porthole and saw an arm, a fierce face: a copper-green woman towering over our ship. She was Liberty, and this was New York Harbor. I was safe, or I thought I was.

My American Movies

FROM THE *GUADALUPE*'S DECK, passengers were waving and calling out to their loved ones on the pier. I hid behind a cluster of passengers and observed my fiancé unseen. Who was that man, so serious in a navy-blue suit, craning his neck? His mother, elegant in tweed, smiled girlishly next to him. Both were scanning the deck. They looked like strangers, both of them. I gave myself orders: *Look happy. Smile.* Vivacious and endearing, I rushed into their arms, willing to do whatever it took to play the model wife—a study I'd begun with other young women at cooking school in Havana.

"In the North," our cooking teacher had told us, "only the Rockefellers have maids." So we'd plunged into complicated recipes for *arroz con pollo* and *pan de gloria*—egg bread—also learning American biscuits and "tuna turnovers."

At home, the woman who came to do our laundry had also given me lessons. My American would be expecting a wife who could starch and iron shirts and sheets, replace buttons, fold socks correctly, and remove stains. Down the gangway I went; kiss, kiss. His quick hug chilled me.

My feelings, the emotions I couldn't muster, were back at La Punta esplanade with Mother, Father and Mama Angélica, with my Miramar neighbors and Fidel, with the farm woman who boiled roots and eggs in her thatched hut. I felt absent at my own great moment; once I'd used up all my *oooohs* I was at a loss for words. I sat in the back seat and listened to them debate which highway to take to Scarsdale, what they'd do to "beat the traffic." My mother-in-law to be told me a child-court judge would perform the civil wedding because I was too young for a regular judge, and then, *wink wink:* "After the civil ceremony, you're married! You don't have to wait for the church wedding."

"Oh, no, no, I'll wait for the real wedding," I said quickly.

"I've got news for you, sweetie," she retorted. "The civil wedding *is* the real wedding."

I was a Catholic. I knew better—or I thought I did.

✳   ✳   ✳

How differently I'd envisioned the consummation of my teenage fantasies, my American dreams. Those dreams, I suppose, had begun with our American-born mother, when my twin brother Roberto and I sat on our small wicker chairs repeating after Mother, who held up a book just like a teacher.

Look, Spot. Oh, look.

Look and see. Oh, see.

Spot, Mother said; *Espot,* we repeated, and I was already in love with the black-and-white Spaniel, with the words that sounded so lovely and were so easy to say.

See, oh see Mother and Dick and Jane.

When Mother sang us to sleep with her quirky lullaby—

Mister Frog went a-courtin' 'n he did ride, uh-huh;

Mister Frog went a-courtin' 'n he did ride,
with a sword and a pistol by his side, uh-huh

—she sent me over the moon along with the cow, the cat and the fiddle.

In my teens, I was a Cuban moth circling the American flame. Life was a potent cocktail of ingredients from *el Norte*: MGM, *True Romances, Silver Screen,* American music on our Havana radio, and my Cuban-American school.

A steady portion of my allowance went to the cash register of Miramar Grocery's magazine annex, where I bought my raw materials: *Archie and Veronica, Seventeen,* movie magazines. The rest of my money was for matinee tickets at Teatro Miramar, three blocks from home, where my American dreams picked up scripts and soundtracks. I used to sing "Tea for Two," "True Love" or "Love Is a Many-Splendored Thing" as I walked home along Quinta Avenida after the matinee—and so I became the young American woman I'd just seen on screen.

School gave me two more American idols. Ruston Academy's headmaster James Baker taught twelfth graders "language in thought and action" or, as he put it, "how to *think* about language." My boyfriend Evelio, the movie star of our class, rolled his eyes when he heard that phrase. *It's too hot to think about language,* his attitude announced. *Why do we have to think about something we've been using forever?*

Mr. Baker furrowed his brow. "Language," he said with impatience, "doesn't just happen. We *make* language. If you don't *know* language, then some day someone is going to herd you like sheep." His message got through just in time. Months after graduation, we were picking apart Fidel's marathon speeches.

Right up there with Jim Baker in my American pantheon was our English teacher Colette Thurman, a soft-spoken, bottle-green-eyed apparition who spoke to no one in particular. She walked the corridors as if in a trance, and dressed in all-American frontier clothing: ankle-length calico skirts, beaded moccasins, turquoise beads. In our just-so Havana school, where teachers wore impeccable linen dresses, pearls and high heels, her attire was a lesson in personal freedom. I coveted her style, and even more I coveted her English when she read aloud to us from Poe, Hemingway or Whitman. The day she stood beside me at the sea and whispered, "Ahhlga, have you ever noticed the ocean is never the same?" a mallet hit me between the eyes and stars went running around my head, as in *Tom and Jerry.*

I wanted that kind of unperturbed independence. I also wanted to step into those summer-camp ads I used to inhale from Sunday editions of *The New York Times.* In catalogs I ordered from New Hampshire, I experienced a world quite far from Havana—a world of log cabins and pine trees, of teenage girls wielding bows and arrows, taking horses over jumps, carrying canoes on their heads. The girls had camp-songs, too.

The cookies that they gave us,
They say are mighty fine.
One rolled off the table
And killed a friend of mine.

Those girls were unencumbered, while we had to sit just so, wear just-so clothes, walk like ladies and not touch our brothers' BB guns; otherwise we'd be labeled *marimachas,* macho-girls. I begged my parents to advance me a year's allowance for summer camp. Instead they sent my brother Roberto.

But not long afterward, I got what I wanted when Mother, Roberto and I went on a Greyhound tour of the Southwest. *That* was the real United States. On Bourbon Street in New Orleans, we watched strippers twirl their tassels clockwise and counter-clockwise as Mother gasped in horror. At Flagstaff, Arizona, I went riding with a wrangler across the prairie under a full moon; our horses flinched at the tumblin' tumbleweeds. In San Francisco, an enormous black chef wiped his hands on a checkered apron, sat down at a piano and gave out boogie-woogie in falsetto. Best of all, from my Greyhound window I had a vision to pierce any cowgirl's heart: an American cowboy in denim and his palomino loping along the highway. When I saw those two, I leaned against the window and crooned, "Happy Trails to You."

❋   ❋   ❋

That same year of 1955, right after Christmas, the American flame drew near to the moth's habitat when two of Mother's American friends, vacationing in Cuba, paid us a visit at Uncle Miguel's farm.

Real Americans! As their car came up the farmhouse driveway, flanked by two rows of blazing red poinsettias, I imagined we were all inside an American movie, *my* American movie, and this was one of the Cuban scenes, the big family on the porch ready and waiting.

If we cut back to the preparations, the soundtrack would be Spanish voices talking loudly. Some of us are sweeping dead June bugs off the porch; others are polishing the dining table until it shines, then placing a dish with guavas, avocados and mangos in the center. We remove loose hairs from the cowhide covers of our rustic *taburete* dining-room chairs. We brush the dog, shoo scorpions out of the dark corners, check the bathroom soap in case it has teeth-marks left by mice, and make sure the special toilet-paper dispenser plays the *Blue Danube* waltz when you pull on the roll. For the main course we are featuring six guinea hens, hunted by Uncle Miguel, which we've plucked and gutted by the light of a hissing Coleman. Uncle Miguel plunges the naked blue-gray birds into chocolate sauce, stirring and tasting with reverence.

Flash forward five years: just before sailing to New York, I ask Miguel for the guinea-hen recipe. Perhaps my new family will enjoy it. He jots it down, grumbling: "Why should I bother?

Those people in the United States, they don't even know what guinea hens are. When they're hungry over there, they just open a can."

And now flash forward to the future: Tío Miguel must also leave Cuba, and "those people in the United States," the ignorant ones, are to become his neighbors, then his doctors and nurses in Coral Gables. One day, and for good, he'll be buried next to them in Florida soil.

※　※　※

Our American guests opened the car doors, looked at our thatched-roof *bohío* and said in breathtaking American English: *Hel-lo, dar-ling, oh, my, my, don't you look LOVE-ly! And who is this young LAY-dy!* The man's English was affable and playful. He gave me a riddle to solve: "How much wood would a woodchuck chuck if a woodchuck could chuck wood?" No matter how often he repeated the riddle, I didn't get it.

The woman's English had an edge. Whenever she didn't quite understand something, she made a sound—*unh-HUNH*—as if to warn the world she was no fool. But she didn't have to be smart, at least not in my book, because she was a dead ringer for Hedy Lamarr. And she had this fantastic, totally American name: "Dot." They were Ed and Dot. How American could you get?

I led them away toward the guava tree where my horse was tethered. I needed them all to myself because I wanted them to fall in love with me. "Meet Sultán. Go ahead, pet him." While they fussed over my horse—I'd shampooed him just before—my winged black high-tops flew me into the kitchen. I grabbed a Domino sugar-cube box and walked back out, shaking it to make Sultán neigh. "Spread out your palm really flat so he can't bite you—like this."

Within an hour, Ed was asking: "How would you like to spend a school year with us in Scarsdale? We have a daughter your age." And Dot: "That would be quite wonderful, hmmmmm?" And

Father: "Let's see." And I, silently: *What's to see? Before they change their minds, say YES! I want to see **real** snow, not the counterfeit flakes we have inside the glass domes on our desks!*

✳   ✳   ✳

By early September 1956, days before my sixteenth birthday and in time for the fall leaves, I was in Scarsdale. By October I was feeling what they called "a nip in the air." Fifty-five degrees Fahrenheit: when I converted that "nip" into centigrade, I realized it was colder than anything I'd known in Havana.

But I loved our Sunday dinner—roast lamb with vegetables browned right in with the meat, apple brown Betty dessert, and a sweet grandma who couldn't quite figure out her hearing aid. On a Sunday that fall, my host family's nephew, an engineering student at a Long Island college, came to dinner. It was love at first sight, and my American movie had begun in earnest.

Scene 1: Sunday dinner. Scene 2: The sixteen-year-old Cuban protagonist and her twenty-year-old beau are at a football game. She's yelling: GO SCARSDALE, BEAT MAMARONECK! MAROON AND WHITE, FIGHT, FIGHT! Scene 3: They drive into "the city" for Dixieland jazz at Carnegie Hall, holding hands. Scene 4: At the movies, his arm is around her shoulder and her head is on his shoulder. Later, at Papa John's Pizza, a candle drips wax down a Chianti bottle covered with straw. Scene 5: The couple is parked on Lovers' Lane. Enter an officer of the law who shines his flashlight at the beau and speaks his obligatory line: "Why don't you take this young lady home?" The MGM lion roars.

Those are the happy scenes. These are some of the tribulations. Dry winter air, dry scalp, nosebleeds and stained pillowcase; Dot is distraught. Frigid walks on Fenimore Road to Scarsdale High School; I've got earaches and chapped hands that bleed inside wool mittens. On the fast cafeteria line, all the choices are alien. At after-school "rough-housing," boys and girls wrestle each other on the living-room floor. To the other girls, I am a "turkey" at best, an irritant at worst. I maroon myself on the sofa until I can slip upstairs to my room, brood about American realities and chide myself for not fitting in.

And back at our *bohío*, who could've known that Ed drinks martini after martini every evening, and gets into fights with Dot—or that I would walk into the kitchen for a glass of milk at the very moment that he's throwing Dot onto the kitchen floor?

※　※　※

I was a misfit, and I ate like one: pizza, after-school hamburgers and chocolate milkshakes. I gorged on the sly, and by Christmas I'd picked up twenty pounds. When I went home for Easter, I tucked my tail between my legs and refused to return to Scarsdale, beau or no beau. The bright American light had singed the moth.

But tortured love is a romantic teenager's aphrodisiac. The courtship resumed by letter and kept up for four years.

※　※　※

A year after Fidel took power, my American *novio* came to Havana. With his crew cut, FBI sunglasses, pale skin and seersucker suit, he was an archetypal *americano.* I liked that, and at the same time I didn't. He was really too different. Even our American classmates at Ruston Academy didn't look or speak like him. At the Plaza de la Catedral, my American blended in so well with tourists that I lost him in the crowd.

I kept his visit a private affair. Maybe I was a little ashamed of him; or maybe I wanted him all to myself. Speaking precisely, I kept him to Mother and myself, since we couldn't go anywhere without a chaperone. Bringing my classmates Elvira and Andrea into our activities would've spoiled things; they would've laughed if they'd seen the water-ballet show I put on for him, smiling my

Esther Williams smile whenever I came up for air. *"¡Oye!"* they would've yelled, "get out of the pool. It's January, freezing cold! Are you *loca?"* Becoming a man's magnificent obsession was something I had to do alone.

The Tropicana nightclub, suffused with the aromas of fine cigars, rum and lime, flowering jasmine, French perfumes and men's cologne, had elegance to burn. It was part open-air and part glass canopy. We could always see the stars at Tropicana. Exuberant vegetation crowded along the walkways between casino, bar and music room. A full orchestra with intense trumpets and chattering bongos blared continuously. Dressed-to-kill dancers danced, while statuesque mulatto women in chandelier headdresses, G-strings and stiletto heels glided by. The humid night air amplified the atmosphere. A girl could lose her virginity, it seemed, just by breathing that air.

My beau and I were the only couple sitting out the dances. He didn't know the steps. As the orchestra went wild, my feet under the table marked out the mambo, the cha-cha, the *guaguancó.* When the orchestra struck up a *danzón,* the sweet, refined step of our ancestors, the men on the floor fussed over their partners; at mid-dance, the couples stopped and the gentlemen waited for the ladies to fan themselves before they took them in their arms again.

As my American smoked his H. Upmann and sipped his "frozen daiquiri"—*What does he mean? All daiquiris are frozen!*—I had a moment of truth. *He is not the man I want at all. I want a man who can lead me in the danzón.*

But then, how wonderful it was to run the palm of my hand back and forth across those bristles of his. Love, indeed, was a many-splendored thing.

❖   ❖   ❖

Father consented, giving his congratulations with a doleful air. The marriage would have to be soon; it was getting harder and

harder to leave Cuba. Mother went into production, making a purple tweed suit for herself to wear to the wedding and a black travel suit for me.

My wedding was announced in *The New York Times* and a clipping of the piece arrived by mail. My picture, the product of several sittings with a Havana photographer, had been doctored for propriety. My neckline and a few bare inches below had been draped over with an image of white cloth; and I felt ashamed, even naked, for being covered up.

Elvira and Andrea helped me shop for the trousseau. Our other friends had either left Cuba or were too caught up in their own personal dramas to offer more than quick congratulations and then ask the urgent question: "When are you leaving?" My engagement was of little consequence next to the all-important matter of going into exile.

※　※　※

Mother had come to Scarsdale for the wedding but Father stayed in Cuba, certain that the government would take over our store and house if he left. My brother Roberto, who'd been studying at the Colorado School of Mines since before the triumph of the Revolution, was there to give me away. I wasn't sure what I wanted. "Go around again," I asked the limo driver, and we circled St. James Anglican Church while I proposed to my brother that I flee with him to Colorado. "*Ay, mi hermana,* you've got to go into that church," was all he said.

Mama Angélica's mother-of-pearl rosary was wound around my wrist. I was in the short satin gown and bouffant veil that Mother had picked out for me. Down the aisle I went on my brother's arm, strangers to the left and strangers to the right. Women in hats and men in dark suits whispered compliments. Everything was foreign: the pale people, the dark Protestant church, the musicians' pompous trumpets. "Trumpet Voluntary,

Olga's Uncle Miguel & Aunt
Consuelo, c. 1940

Olga's engagement photo

Olga's mother, 1935

Henry Purcell," the program read. The relative who photographed the wedding returned to my in-laws empty-handed weeks later. Every picture of the wedding had come back blank. I wasn't surprised.

La primera noche, the "first night" that teenagers in Cuba romanticize—no, glorify—was in a Manhattan hotel room with a close-up view of the brick wall opposite. I would have wanted fields, a stream and flowers. In the bathroom I changed into my vaporous white nightgown, brushed my teeth and emerged ready for something. All I knew was that there would be blood.

Next morning, we took a yellow cab to Greenwich Village. *My first breakfast as a married woman,* I observed to myself in the back seat of the cab. I braced myself then for what I was about to do. What choice did I have? The dark Protestant church had unhinged me. If I didn't inveigle him now, then when could I? Never again would he be this taken with me. Speaking softly, I sent my question across the table: "Would you let me bring up our children, when we have them, in the Catholic Church?"

First, silence—and then, his face ablaze, came the roaring assault. "Don't you ever, *ever....* You damn Papist!"

His face lunged at mine as if to penetrate it. The dining room fell silent. A man at the next table threw down his napkin and pushed back his chair as if getting ready to intercede.

Who was this man I'd married? I remembered "paranoid rage" from clinical psych, felt horror and realized that bad things could happen to me. I wondered, too, about my own self-deception, my deviousness. I was marooned inside my American dreams. I had no one to look after me except this man. The next morning we took the Connecticut Turnpike all the way to a black-shingled ranch house on RFD319, North Stonington, in the backwoods of Connecticut.

Norse Estoningto—Nort Tonyngton—Norsetonington—North Thtonington—the name was unpronounceable. The place had no sidewalks. Cows were knee-deep in dung across the road. The snows began, and so did the silence. I had nothing to do all day but push the vacuum cleaner, wax the floors, iron and stare out the window. The frigid wind wrapping itself around the corners of the house was the only sound I heard. The only movements I saw were the dry branches, the mail car, the *Pennysaver* delivery lady, and the twice-a-week milkman I watched for so that we could talk a little. Once I offered him lunch but he said, "Thank you, missus. I've got my route to do."

And what about the torrid love scenes Elvira and Andrea had acted out while I tried on vaporous nightgowns in El Encanto? "Whorish," my husband called my nightgowns. It was a new word to me. He preferred to lock himself in the bathroom for half-hour showers. The day he forgot to lock the door, I peeked in and saw his silhouette quivering behind the shower curtain. So that's what he was doing. Next, I set out to uncover how he spent those evenings when he sequestered himself down in the basement workshop. I heard him scrambling at the sound of my steps on the stairs and found him red-faced, rag in hand. He was zipping up his pants; a copy of *Playboy* was spread open on his workbench.

I ate ice cream by the pint, and the food left over from our dinner plates. By spring thaw, I'd gained thirty pounds. I gave up trying to pray. I supposed I'd forfeited the right with my Protestant wedding.

Saturdays and Sundays he catalogued his *National Review* magazines, stuffed pennies into little tubes, washed and waxed the car, cleaned and oiled his guns, went looking for rats to shoot at the town dump. Every few weeks there'd be a trip to Sears, where he inspected wrenches and screwdrivers, drills and power tools. Sunday afternoons were for TV football and liquor. We went to one party the first year. He thought he'd seen me flirting. On the way home, in the car, he reached for the back of my head as if to caress me and smashed my forehead against the windshield. "I'll kill you if I ever see you flirting again."

I fell silent with dread that he would kill me then and there. The glass cracked straight across, but my face showed no bruising. *Maybe I'm strong enough to stand up to him. Maybe this is a sign.*

Some weekends, the gloom lifted. His parents drove up from Scarsdale bringing loud conversation, Danish pastries, enormous steaks, homemade syrup for their Old Fashioneds, and lots of liquor they speedily downed before hurrying back to the kitchen to "freshen up" their drinks, hanging on to doorframes to steady their way. Back in the living room, they plunged into reminiscences of family tragedies, growing teary-eyed over "my poor brother John" or "Cousin Billy who committed suicide." Withal, I was grateful for my blustery mother-in-law who called me "doll," and for her boozy stage-whisper to my father-in-law: "Don't you love the way she's always kissing us?"

Calls to Mother and Father in Havana were expensive, and my husband pointed at his watch as I spoke. For three years, those long-distance conversations were all the Spanish I spoke. "I love the snow, Papi. Today it was over my head after I shoveled the driveway. Imagine that." "Do you still remember Havana?" Father always asked.

Papi, I remember the Malecón. *Did you ever notice it's an ultramarine blue crescent? The* Malecón *and the Old City,* La Habana Vieja, *are what I think of most. I can name its narrow streets, but ours, O'Reilly, is the crown jewel. The Casa Karman store, Calle O'Reilly. You worked too hard there, buried yourself in work, never took vacations. Thank you for the summer job you gave me after I graduated from Ruston. O'Reilly Street turned me into a real* habanera. *Do you remember our ride to work early morning along the* Malecón?

The city was wide-awake, the streets full; people rushed to catch buses; food-cart peddlers hawked oranges; corner cafés served customers who demanded *café con leche;* merchants rolled up their metal grills and swept the sidewalks. The buildings along those narrow streets were a continuum of life: stores at ground level, apartments upstairs where families kept potted geraniums and caged canaries. Children in school uniform ran down the stairs and out the door, pieces of bread still in their fists. The echo of so many footsteps bouncing off walls intensified the feeling of life.

Efectos Eléctricos, the sign above our store window read— "Electrical Appliances." We had Victrolas, gooseneck lamps, batteries you imported from that man in Dallas who'd come to the house for dinner. The soot was everywhere in Casa Karman, centuries of soot, even inside the drawer where you kept the ceramic fuses. My flannel dusting cloth wiped your appliances clean of their pulverized history; for dust was all that remained of the Spanish galleons that docked at our harbor four hundred years ago on their way back home, filled with booty from the New World for Queen Isabella and King Ferdinand. They were ships bearing gold and silver, sheaves of tobacco, Indian slaves and parrots. The work at Casa Karman was so boring that I had to make up those histories.

Remember how people raced to finish business before the two-hour lunch break? How customers banged on the side of the wooden orange cart and barked at the peddler, *"¡Dale, chico!* Hurry it up, boy!" But the man turned a deaf ear, chose the next orange with ceremony, trapped it inside the vise with infinite calm, shaved off the peel and inspected it slowly as if saying: *No one will rush me. I am the orange man. This is my work; this is my art.* I wanted to be like that orange man someday—exacting and faithful to my work. No one would rush me; no one would tell me how to peel my oranges.

You and I walked side by side along the narrow sidewalk at lunchtime, past the minuscule Parque Alvear and Ernest Hemingway's El Floridita bar, where you stopped to buy a noontime paper, *¡Alerta!* or *El Crisol,* so that you could spread it across the front seat of the car because it would be broiling inside the

Ford we'd left on the Prado although the parking attendant who snapped his chamois and called you *Doctor* would have rolled all the windows down. While you paid for the paper, I inhaled the air oozing from the Floridita: seafood, garlic, cigarette smoke, lime juice, rum. Laughter broke out among many excited voices, along with the sound of the Osterizer that might have been whipping up Hemingway's daiquiri. I wouldn't have dreamt of asking you to invite me to lunch at the Floridita although I was almost eighteen years old and worldly, or so I thought. You were too humble, too incapable of self-indulgence. Not me; in my imagination I went there every day. I saw myself seated at my table, lighting a Kool, looking around while the tuxedoed bartender made and delivered my daiquiri. Then I went back to the Malecón and on to Mama Angélica and Papa Karman's house, where every day for forty years you had your lunch.

Back at Casa Karman, as the day sped to a close, I hurried to finish my job so I could sneak out and walk the neighborhood streets: *Lamparilla*—Little Lamp, *Aguacate*—Avocado, *Obispo*— Bishop. I adored the thrill of feeling myself a real *habanera*. What a gift it was to belong to a city so seamlessly that I felt invisible. Along the dark, narrow streets I could catch a glimpse of ocean and indigo sky, and the blue light made me gasp at its fleeting beauty.

❖ ❖ ❖

My husband kept his single-edged razor blades in the bathroom cabinet. I lay them in a perfect row on the bathtub rim, climbed into the tub with my clothes on and reached for a blade.

"Come on, put those razors away. Come on. You can try again tomorrow."

Whose voice was it? Who was making me rewrap the razors?

That voice was there next day and the day after. Steady, gentle, it found me and kept me alive.

From Wolf to Wolf

WHEN MY DAUGHTER WAS BORN, Dr. McKeon, the Scottish obstetrician whose English I rarely understood, laid her across my chest, where she mewed like a hoarse kitten. "I'm crying too," I told Carla and held on to her.

Returning from the hospital, rounding the corner onto our street in small-town Mystic, where we'd lately moved, I saw my predicament: twenty-two years old, trapped in a heartless marriage, a prisoner on a foam-rubber donut. My world seemed so small: a brown-shingled ranch house where I played with a dustpan, iron, floor-mop, window cleaner, waxer and polisher. While Carla nursed I listened to *Aïda:* "*O patria mia, mai più, mai più ti rivedrò!* Oh, my homeland, I will never, never see you again!" I had something in common with Aïda; I felt I was being buried alive.

And then came the bombshell. My neighbor Eleanor appeared at the door with a book. "You've got to read this." It was *The Feminine Mystique* by Betty Friedan.

A woman ... who has ... no purpose ... making her stretch and grow beyond that small score of years in which her body can fill its biological function is committing a kind of suicide.

I determined to save myself the only way I knew. I would go back to college.

I ran next door to Claire for courage, but Claire looked up from the laundry she was folding and said, "A mother doesn't run off and leave her child. No woman in this neighborhood abandons her children."

Her blunt speaking frightened me—and then it liberated me.

Connecticut College, less than a half-hour's drive from Mystic, was another planet, where forbidding stone buildings perched on a privileged hilltop above New London and Long Island Sound, dominating land and sea. Having lost my college in Cuba when Castro closed it three years earlier, could I now be "American college material"? How much would Connecticut College cost? What would I do with the baby?

I crossed the New London Bridge with Carla, and up we went onto a sacred ground where young women, so young in their sweaters and skirts, walked in and out of buildings with purpose, their strides telling the world *we are going places.* A flock of them played field hockey across from the library; their coach ran alongside blowing her whistle, yelling, "pinny, non-pinny, GIRLS!!!"

Look at them. Each one sprang full-grown from American soil and walked into Conn College as if it belonged to her. Who am I? I'm nobody. They'll banish me.

In the parking lot, I leafed through the catalog to see what I'd be missing: psychology, history, Spanish, botany, art, creative writing, horseback riding.

Horseback riding?

The others I could let go, but that one was too much to lose. Back in Mystic, I dialed the college; someone gave me a date for an interview. I'd find a babysitter. If need be, I'd make one out of clay.

"And how much would it cost?" "Twelve-thirty," answered a heavy-set man in a dark suit. *Twelve-thirty? Why is he telling me the time?* I checked the wall clock: ten-ten. *Oh. He means dollars. Well, that finishes it.*

On a Sunday afternoon during TV football, my husband, having gone into the kitchen to "freshen his drink," called out to me. As soon as I was next to him he dragged his index finger across the counter, looked at his fingertip and made a face. "It's greasy. Maybe it's because you're Cuban or something."

I looked down at the floor, saying nothing. On Monday I registered for a course at Connecticut College: English literature, three hours a week.

* * *

The girl-women in short skirts, knee socks and buttery twin sweaters might have popped right out of *Seventeen*. Vivacious— more than vivacious, perky—they called to each other in staccato American phrases: "Boat out of the water Saturday!" "Got a train schedule?" After morning class, they rushed to the mailboxes looking for invitations to Yale weekends addressed to them in manly script. When the invitations came, they read them out loud and whined: "What am I going to wear?" "Who wants to share a cab to the station?" "Amyyyyy, borrow your camel coat, pleeeeease?"

I saw myself all wrong: purple-, black-, turquoise- and magenta poodle-textured Montgomery Ward's car coat, a wad of S&H Green Stamps in one pocket and Zwieback crumbs in the other. No matter how often I reminded myself of why I was here—to get a diploma so I could leave my husband; to create my life or fail in the attempt—it smarted to be invisible and friendless.

Then again, what did I care about fitting in with teenagers? My eyes were on a bigger prize: Professor Mackie Jarrell, her fuchsia suit and sling-back shoes, her nasal voice modulated by French cigarettes and fine scotches; the magician/professor who brought famous dead writers to class and held one-way conversations with them. How nimble was her thinking; what a cliffhanger it was to follow her line of argument! Mackie Jarrell made it possible for me to leap clear out of my unhappy skin.

From that very first class at which she announced, with a dollop of derision in her voice, "This is a survey course, from Beowulf to Virginia Woolf," she fascinated me. A general twitter had broken out when she said that. I didn't get the humor. Beowulf, English author; Virginia Woolf, English author; what was funny except perhaps wolf and wolf? I had yet to discover that Beowulf was no author. But where was the harm? After all, I'd come to college to learn.

Epiphany struck when Mackie closed her copy of *Beowulf* and introduced me to Geoffrey Chaucer. She stepped out from behind the lectern and came to a dead halt in front of the class as if contacting something far away, something only she could see, way beyond the classroom, beyond Palmer Library, beyond Arnold Arboretum. And then: "Whan that Aprill with his shoures soote/ The droughte of March hath perced to the roote," reciting line after line Chaucer's prologue all the way to "whan that they were secke." I thought I would faint. The music, that voice like an oboe, the words she'd worn smooth over the years, as smooth as the beads on Mama Angélica's mother-of-pearl rosary, all of it was her birthright. She was entitled to recite Chaucer; Chaucer was hers to command. *Some day I'm going to sound like Mackie Jarrell. Some day I'm going to make "melodye" like those little birds, the "smale fowles," who sleep all night "with open ye."*

After class I walked straight through the busy mailroom, turned left into the small college store and bought a recording of *The Canterbury Tales*. As soon as Carla was asleep in her crib, I sat on the floor next to the record player, lifted the needle and played the Prologue, repeating and imitating every nuance in every word of the first eighteen lines. If I studied with all my might and mastered those words, I could make English my second birthright.

It wouldn't be easy. Whenever I spoke up in class, I seemed to miss the point; after a string of reaaaalllys and perhaaaaapses, Mackie moved on to the next student who, expressionless and speaking with a tightened jaw, gave an unintelligible yet smart-sounding answer. The day she discussed "papers" and the MLA format I was pretty sure I didn't belong there.

I was no reader. I'd never read anything I hadn't been told to read, except *Bonjour tristesse* and *The Feminine Mystique.* Unlike Mother, who used to fall asleep in her hammock at siesta time with a book on her chest, I fell asleep listening to baseball over the radio, visualizing Minnie Miñoso's plays. Growing up in Cuba had been an outdoor experience—ocean and farm. We swam and snorkeled, rowed and sailed, chased lobsters back into their caves. I rode my taffy-colored Sultán far away from the farm, all by myself; I helped Tío Miguel with his "farm projects" such as waging underground chemical warfare against leaf-cutter ants. Indoors was for eating and sleeping, watching Fidel Castro on television, dancing to our records of Celia Cruz, Barbarito Diez, Bill Haley and the Comets. So I felt humbled when Mackie told me, "I read everything. Even the writing on cereal boxes while I'm having breakfast."

If reading was not second nature, writing was. I had plunged right into the English writing assignments at Ruston, where teachers invited us to "tell about our lives" although they were merciless graders whose hawk-eyes looked out for sentence fragments, faulty logic, comma splices, dangling participles and other assorted refuse. Then, swaggering like John Wayne, they flung our compositions back at us with a grunt, and we found a minus grade right next to the evil word "mechanics." A or A-minus in "content" and minus 10 or worse in "mechanics" wasn't rare for me, but little by little I'd managed to make the two grades look alike.

I followed Mackie to her office and, face burning, asked for a definition of "a paper." She seemed flustered, and did something with her hair, "Whellll … it's just an essay, really. The bibliography will be helpful, I'm sure!" I scanned the voluminous bibliography and asked the question that professors despise: "Do we have to read all of them?" She ushered me to the door. "You'll do fiiiine."

All wasn't fiiiine at the library when I tried to borrow the bibliography books. "On closed reserve," the librarian said. *What does she mean, closed reserve?* I explained to her that they were for us, for Mrs. Jarrell's students. The librarian looked at me with impatience, and I saw myself trapped in a heartless marriage. Then came the offer: she would allow me to pick up the books at closing time, but I had to bring them back before she opened in the morning. I'd have to travel thirty miles to get the books, but I'd have the entire night to read.

In Mystic, the silent house kept me company. "Keep reading. Don't look at the clock," it whispered to me like an invisible chorus. In those books, the famous dead authors came alive and taught me how to read.

Mackie returned my first essay with a big letter *A* and a note: "This paper is graduate-school quality." Although I didn't quite understand the comment, I blew a kiss to my Ruston teachers. A star-tipped wand had touched my hair, and I took a giant step in the direction of freedom.

In late spring 1964, Mother decided to leave Cuba all by herself, hoping her departure would force Father to leave. I hadn't seen her in more than three years. I'd have a granddaughter ready and waiting for her. I began to teach Carla some Spanish words, and I bought matching pink dresses for us to wear to the airport. By noon the day of her flight, Carla and I were in starched pink, ready for the drive from Mystic to Idlewild. I looked for my husband. He was in shorts and a T-shirt, garden hose in hand, washing the car. He looked away from us and kept washing the car, shampooed the hubcaps, polished the chrome. If he didn't stop at once, we'd be late. Mother would find herself unwelcome, alone and frightened. I pranced around the car begging, offering to help him finish the job; but he made believe he didn't hear or see me.

Mother had been waiting for an hour when we found her sitting on a bench, her swollen feet resting on a single suitcase. I forgot my anger, snatched Carla up and ran to her. Her hands were shaking when she reached out for Carla. In four years, my mother had become more like a daughter than a mother.

When we were alone in the room I'd arranged for her in Mystic, she asked for a pair of scissors. She took her old Chinese slippers out of the suitcase, handed them to me, took them back and began to rip the seams open. "I saved this for your college." Out of the soles Mother pulled hundred-dollar bills, one after another.

For the first time in more than three years, I was speaking Spanish at home. I was majoring in Spanish at Connecticut College because psychology demanded many hours of lab work, and I needed to be there for my toddler. So I'd be a high-school teacher instead of a clinical psychologist. An American professor, Argyll Pryor Rice, taught most of my Spanish literature courses. Like me, she was off to the side of the college mainstream. I befriended her, and she became a guardian angel who changed my life.

"You could be a high-school Spanish teacher if you like, but you really belong in graduate school. Wouldn't you like to be a college professor?"

She helped me prepare for the Graduate Record Exam and fill out applications to Harvard, Yale and UConn. She told me about the Woodrow Wilson Fellowship and looked over my application before I mailed it to New York City.

I was one of two Conn College students who made the Woodrow Wilson Fellowship finals. The other student's mother, a professor of Italian at the college, drove us to the city for our interviews. Sitting in the back seat of her Mercedes, I wondered about my chances. My mother hadn't even finished high school. Father had started to work at Casa Karman in his teens; no college. My family background would surely doom me.

The dignified receptionist called me in first. She led me into a cozy room wainscoted in dark wood, with Oriental rugs, overstuffed leather chairs and a fire burning in the fireplace. Three men in handsome dark suits got to their feet, sat down again and began the interview—an oral exam of sorts. Abruptly one of them picked up a glass ashtray and said: "Your honors thesis is about the poet Antonio Machado. Describe this ashtray the way Machado would."

I wanted to laugh. They'd invited me all the way to Manhattan just so I could impersonate Antonio Machado. What fun! I picked up the ashtray, forgot who I was and where I'd come from. I began to improvise a first-person story linking the glass object to the windows of my classroom in Seville and to what I could see outdoors: the tiled patio, the lemon tree in bloom. I myself was watching over my students but dreaming of my beloved Leonor, whose eyes reflected light just as the cut-glass ashtray was reflecting the light from the fireplace in the wood-paneled room. The make-believe carried me, and everything I said was dripping with the poet's vocabulary. When I finished and put the ashtray back on the table, I puffed up inside, for I knew I had become Machado.

Riding home on the Connecticut Turnpike, I sobered up and the performance came back to me in a horrible reflux. What a poor pastiche it had been! What a profanation! I could forget all about that fellowship.

Days or maybe weeks later, the phone rang. It was Judy, a neighbor. "Congratulations. I just saw your picture in *The Day*." I didn't understand. "Didn't you get your paper yet? There's an article about you winning a fellowship." Then came Judy's clincher: "Gee, I was surprised. You don't look that smart."

Harvard, Yale and UConn sent acceptance letters. Carla and I wouldn't die of hunger. The Romance Languages chairman at Harvard, Professor Rogers, called. "I'm here with Professors Marichal and Anderson-Imbert, and we'd like to invite you to come to Harvard, but we want you to know that Harvard doesn't work around babysitter schedules."

"You're last because you're summa." Conn College Commencement, 1966

Babysitter schedules? Might as well return the fellowship; you'll never make it. But it was too late for me to reverse. I'd crossed my Rubicon. I had no way back.

❧ ❧ ❧

What a morning for an outdoor commencement: full sun, sea breeze rising up the hill to Conn College, Argyll fluttering around me, Carla running around in her pink cotton dress with a big bow in back. My husband seemed proud enough; he suspected nothing. I felt guilt and dread at what lay ahead, but I stoked up the memories of his cruelty and kept myself on task. Handsome Kingman Brewster, Yale's president, had come all the way from New Haven to deliver the commencement address and hand out the diplomas. *My very own Yalie.* Time to line up; the professor in charge led me to the end of the procession. "Why am I last? Aren't we going alphabetically?" The impatient answer came from a student: "You're last because you're summa. Summa is last in line."

And then, when it was over, the students' voices, playful as flutes or piccolos, rose up to Conn College heaven: WE MADE IT! I'LL COME SEE YOU! I MEAN IT!

My instrument was a somber 'cello. I'd won my freedom, and very soon I'd use it. Commencement was my signal. In the three years that had gone by since that day with my husband and the kitchen counter, I had plotted my escape.

We were moving to the Boston area, where my husband had gotten a job transfer he welcomed. "Just think, there'll be new people to hate ... I mean meet," he'd commented, turning red. First, for me, would come six weeks of Latin summer school so I could pass Harvard's entrance exam. That would make a year of Latin in six weeks; but it was little compared to changing the life of a three-year-old girl with a big pink bow in back. I would pass Harvard's Latin exam, and then I would leave my husband.

Veritas

THE CHARLES RIVER MEANDERS into Cambridge. *Meandro,* a tenth-grade geography word that *Doctora* Josefina Esteban had explained in her deadly nasal monotone: *"Meandros* tell a river's age like wrinkles on a person's face." I'd noticed *la doctora* had no wrinkles, but her wavy salt-and-pepper hair was one *meandro* after another.

At the wheel of my vintage electric-blue VW beetle, I wondered out loud: *Am I still a young river, or has life slowed me down as it has the Charles?*

Young, I told myself and stepped on the gas, leaning into the curves. I was twenty-six, and the Sixties were in full flower. But there was another me, and I knew her well: tired, grim, weighted down with responsibility, about to dismantle a marriage and make a three-year-old suffer. My financial future was bleak; and now I must secretly search for a cheap apartment in an unfamiliar city.

The red brick bridges over the Charles River came into view and took my breath away. Students were walking along the banks or pedaling ten-speed bicycles in bright summer jerseys that looked like banners to the wind. A shell sped by with a tiny coxswain yelling into his tiny megaphone; a dog leapt for a Frisbee and landed on a picnic. On the other bank, sycamores reflected sunlight up and down their trunks, a soft yellow sheen glowing on their mottled bark. A red brick hamlet lay just beyond. White steeples, filigreed garden gates, dogwood, laurel, azalea—this was Harvard.

The uneven Cambridge sidewalks, ancient in feeling, sent history shooting up my calves. Soon I would memorize the places where bricks protruded or formed treacherous hollows, and I would wager I could walk along Mass Ave. blindfolded. For now I stumbled, distracted by so much life in a place quite unlike my small Connecticut town. Schoenhoff's window was chock-full of foreign books. Leavitt & Pearce tobacconist, where I bought my first pack of Gauloises, was scented with an aroma I remembered from home. That perfume had been trapped inside the H. Upmann cigar box I'd used as a pencil case in grade school. The genteelly seedy Hayes-Bickford's cafeteria became the first place in the United States where I overheard a Spanish conversation in public. *No cabe duda*, a man wearing a beret was telling his bouffant companion in periwinkle blue linen—"no doubt about it." At the main news kiosk, I bought Mother and Father a postcard to show them exactly where I stood: under the clock in Harvard Square. I also bought a notebook with a crimson *H* and Harvard's motto— *our* motto—on the cover: *veritas*, truth.

The walk around Cambridge was my timid approach to the tall iron gate separating Harvard Yard from the rest of the universe. When finally I dared to cross the threshold, all traffic became inaudible. A sudden hush: I was in The Yard. How serene, how intimate was the shade; how majestic were the old trees. Out of the silence rose a hum, a delicate thrum. It was the blood running through my temples and announcing my resurrection. I'd come back from the dead. This blood-music was the music of the living. *No cabe duda.*

I wanted to give the music to my daughter Carla, but I doubted my honesty. Except at odd moments of respite, I didn't believe I deserved a rebirth more than she deserved a home with two parents; and I punished myself. *You've just moved your family to the Boston area, barely settled into a house in Newton, and you're getting ready to move Carla again.* I felt anguish as I watched her at play under the new pine tree. *I'm a cyclone in my daughter's life. I can't go through with this. Who says I have to be happy?*

Could I blame history for this disaster? Could I blame Fidel Castro or my own exile? At times I reviewed my husband's cruelties and found justification. Then I recalled something Mother had told me when I was a teenager: "You're so good at schoolwork and so bad at life." Here I was, a student at Harvard and a failed human being.

At times a fainter voice tried to be heard. *If you stay with this man, you're going to die.* Back and forth went this argument between self-sacrifice and self-preservation.

Peace, when it came, I owed to my summer classmate Margaret, the first single woman I'd befriended in the United States. Her surroundings—-quite a boon after my Mystic ranch house where "art" meant a framed photo of the *Charles W. Morgan,* "last of the wooden whalers"—-included classical music records, copies of Rembrandt drawings, sheepskins on hardwood floors and amber worry-beads from Mykonos. Margaret roasted chicken on Sunday so she wouldn't have to cook during the week, and she didn't need a man to carve thin slices at lunchtime. "Voilà!" she exclaimed on serving a baguette that spilled over with chicken, Brie, apple and Dijon mustard. She played Purcell—"Come, come ye Sons of Art / Come, come away / Tune all your voices and instruments play / To celebrate this triumphant day"—and told me we were *daughters* of art, Harvard daughters of art. We drank iced coffee to stay awake, translated Horace, Catullus and Seneca, repeated Latin cases and deponent verbs.

Margaret's moment of glory came the morning of the Latin

final exam, when she invited Dr. K., our instructor, to lunch at the Spanish restaurant Iruña in the Square. "Just to celebrate the end of the course," she averred. In flashy Spanish, hands flying, we ordered Rioja wine and *sopa de ajo*, with two eggs staring out of the broth—"just for you, Dr. K., special." We regaled him with well-rehearsed Latin puns and aphorisms as we waited for our food. Over espresso and flan, we gave him our message: "*Lingua Latina superanda est*"—*We must pass Latin.* He blushed. The check came; Margaret and I split it. "We passed fair and square," Margaret called to tell me the day our grades arrived in the mail.

That very evening, after Carla was asleep, I informed my husband that we would be separating. His *macho* blood up, he opened the kitchen drawer, looked around for something, didn't find it, reached under the sink, and before I could get out of the way he'd emptied the garbage can on my head.

"If you leave me, I'll kill you!" he hollered.

With wet coffee grounds sticking to my face and hair, I understood clearly that I might die. Everything inside me begged: *No, not now. I can't die now. I'm almost there.* Slowly I backed away, got out the front door and ran to my neighbor's house. Rita rinsed my hair, gave me tea and told me about her friend Anne Sexton while we waited for the lights to go out in my bedroom. When I slipped back into the darkened house, my husband screamed from the top of the stairs: "I'll kill you!"

The movers I'd secretly hired were scheduled for a morning pickup, but that day my husband woke up feeling ill and wondered whether he should stay home. He looked into his bottom eyelid and throat for signs of disease, then said: "What the hell, I'll go to work."

Carla and I rode the moving truck to an unpaved alley in Somerville where I'd rented a $90-a-month apartment. *Look at our funny new toilet, Carla! It's got a water tank up high, a pull-chain. Look, the tub has claw feet! There's a dead mouse right in the oven! Let's bury it!* I did my best to make the place adventurous, while outside the landlord barked at the movers: "Watch it! KAY-ah-ful with that do-ah!"

I had to tell him the truth before the bulk of the furniture was inside the apartment. "Mr. Bettencourt, my husband might come looking for me. He says he wants to kill me. He collects guns. Can we still stay?" Dick Bettencourt looked at me dead on, hitched up his pants, contemplated his tiny strip of lawn and rusted chain-link fence. "Oh, yeah? Just let him try to set foot inside my yahhhhd!"

I swept the "paahlaaah" singing "Alma de roca," while Carla used her Play-Doh to plug up holes in the living-room floor. From now on, our fate would depend on me. I pushed the broom and sang.

✻　✻　✻

The young Boston architect I'd met through Margaret was another reason to sing; but happiness made for an emotional see-saw, joy triggering self-recrimination. Joy with Mark, and up I went. Guilt over Carla, and down I fell. On the downside of the ledger, a big entry was my fear of being destitute. I tallied rent, babysitter, gasoline, car insurance, clothing for two, food for two, textbooks, utilities and "miscellaneous." The sum exceeded my annual income of two thousand dollars made up from scholarship money, child support and Harvard's teaching-fellow stipend.

We lived on "Meat-Plus," powdered milk, bulk-bin cereal reminiscent of cat's chow, and tuna tins. When we shopped for food and Carla lunged for a box of Lucky Charms or a Hostess cupcake, I snapped at her and then reproved myself. To stretch my dollars, I went to Boston's Quincy Market on Saturday mornings, late, after the prices had gone down. I was happy there, listening to the produce vendors cry out: "Help anyone heeaaaahh?" Just steps away was Paul Reveaaahh's statue in front of Old North Church, where Longfellow's hero proclaimed, *"One if by land, and two if by sea."* Among pushcarts and shoppers, I had stepped into history; rather than being a dislocated Cuban, I was an American on hallowed ground. It scarcely mattered that the ground was buried under sawdust, cabbage leaves, mangled beets and carrot tops.

* * *

I had begun to feel settled. Could Harvard and Cambridge be the home I was seeking? I felt legitimate enough when tour buses slowed down in front of Harvard Yard and cameras pointed at me. In my camel miniskirt, black turtleneck and fishnet stockings, briefcase in hand, I must have looked like a native, as natural among Americans as I'd been on the streets of Havana.

The illusion vanished when I walked into Elsie's luncheonette, where a young JFK's autographed photo smiled at customers standing three deep and yelling their orders in a deliberately riotous way: *Tuna on a bulkie! Roast beef on rye, mustard, hold the mayo!* I wasn't yelling. I was too frightened to yell. In Cuba, I had yelled at cafeteria counters all through my girlhood; but this was Cambridge. When the man behind the counter pointed his knife at me with a snarled "Yeah?" I whispered: "Ham and swiss on pumpernickel, without onion, please."

"Ham and swiss on dark!" the man boomed. "And hold the onion—the young lady's got a date!"

I vowed never to return to Elsie's, though I did, many times, trying but failing to master it. Who was I to raise my voice in a luncheonette full of Pilgrims' descendants—Mayflower people born with the right to yell *Tuna on a bulkie?*

I wasn't home. Worse, I couldn't *go* home. Latin American classmates returned to Chile, Colombia or Mexico for the holidays, while I stayed behind and yearned for Cuba. Seeing them leave wasn't as bad as seeing them return with a new poncho or a perforated silver spoon for their fresh supply of *maté* tea. How humble and yet how irreplaceable *home* was; the aroma of Mama Angélica's sandalwood fan, of Evelio's H. Upmann cigar, of

Sultán's fur when I shampooed him, of windfalls under the guava tree. My supplies from home were photos inside a decorative album—photos that would never be replenished. There was no going back. If I wanted Cuba, I'd have to make it up.

So I did, with paper and ink—a paper *patria,* all the *patria* I'd ever have. My Cuba was cobbled from words of José Martí, Julián del Casal, Alejo Carpentier. I seized Cuba wherever I could find it; as in the pages of José Lezama Lima's novel *Paradiso,* which became my Ph.D. thesis topic. I scoured for odds and ends of my country in strips of microfilm that I studied in the basement of Widener Library. Reading old issues of *Ciclón* and *Orígenes* through the tiny microfiche lens was almost, almost, like being in Cuba.

And then, quite suddenly, being at Harvard was almost like being in the streets of Havana. All hell had broken loose over the Vietnam War. Demonstrations had transformed the serene Harvard campus into a battlefield. Students were picketing, occupying buildings and holding "teach-ins" to condemn not just the war but all of American society.

Harvard wasn't paradise, the protesters claimed; it was just another cog in America's capitalist machinery. The student rebels' model for change was the Cuban Revolution. Their idols were Fidel Castro and Che Guevara. Students didn't realize that Fidel and Che would have banned their protests and put them all in prison. I was Alice in Wonderland falling down the rabbit hole.

The morning of my Latin finals, a picket line blocked the steps to the exam room in Sever Hall. Bob, a classmate, was pumping a placard with a red-and-black portrait of Che Guevara. Seeing Che's scraggly beard and beret made me dizzy. When Bob spotted me about to cross the line, he harangued with gusto: "*You, obsolete Cuban, gusana, worm!*"

Students glared. *Will she cross?* In spite of the dread, I told myself: *Cross it! Go! You're free. Go!* Inside Sever, I grabbed my "blue book" and started with a trembling hand to write Latin translations.

Some hours later, at the Café Pamplona in Harvard Square, Bob the insurrectionist, mouth full of croissant and cappuccino, announced to fellow students: "When the shooting starts, I'll shoot you dead if you're in the wrong trenches."

The student hero was a croissant-and-cappuccino revolutionary. Had I pigeonholed Bob? Sure I had; but my dread was genuine. Where would my small daughter and I flee if the United States collapsed? *You naïve Americans, don't you realize a whole country can go under? Mine did.*

✦ ✦ ✦

In spite of civil unrest and my own anguish, Harvard seemed as luminous as the ocean when the sun turns its surface to goldleaf. On one such morning, our *Don Quijote* professor, who paced like a caged leopard when he lectured, told us about Quijote's defeat. Suddenly, Steve Gilman's voice cracked. He stopped speaking, removed his fogged eyeglasses, wiped them with his handkerchief and set them down on the table. Waiting for him to continue, I mourned for Quijote and for all those who think their dreams have come to nothing.

Some afternoons, driving home along the banks of the Charles and still brimming with what Professor Lida had said in class, I imagined a walled-in patio where St. Teresa, St. John of the Cross and Federico García Lorca walked round and round reciting to each other. "The Lord is as near to you as your cooking-pots— *Entre los pucheros anda el Señor,*" St. Teresa said, while St. John told of flames consuming his soul without causing pain. García Lorca spoke with his hands as he described Antoñito, the jasmine-and-olive-skinned gypsy with carnations in his voice. "Come, join us!" the three of them called out to me, and I entered the circle to find a homeland where I'd always be welcome, a *patria* that even Fidel Castro couldn't decimate.

✦ ✦ ✦

He's the man I should have married at twenty. I was twenty-seven and Carla five. A year and a half later, 1970, our son arrived. Before his birth, we'd wondered which name to choose: Sam, Nathan, Max, Nathaniel. Six weeks before the due-date, Mark, Carla and I agreed: "It's Nathaniel!"

No sooner had I spoken his name than warm water gushed down my legs; and in a few hours, Nathaniel—*gift of God* in Hebrew—had come to us. We brought him home in the fire-engine-red bunting Mother had made for him. On the ride back to Newton, Mark took the Charles River curves ever so gingerly.

✻   ✻   ✻

After two years of courses, I must spend a third "reading for general examinations." Professor Anderson-Imbert took umbrage when we asked him for a reading list. "There's no list! *Se lee todo*—one reads everything." He tugged at his vest. "How could anyone assume a Harvard Ph.D. was a matter of a reading list!" So I read "everything" and re-read it the week before exams—a week uncombed, barefoot, stepping around books in my study like an egret in a stream of stones, getting ready for sixteen hours of "writtens" and an oral exam where I would be at the firing wall and Professors Lida, Anderson-Imbert and Marichal would discharge their questions at will.

I moved through the two exam days in a trance, above fatigue. After the oral exam Professor Marichal looked at the floor, avoiding my eyes, and whispered, "High Pass." He shook my hand and fled into his office. I'd missed Honors. We were both embarrassed. A silent beer with Mark derailed self-punishment, and in the days that followed I treated myself to small but magnificent pleasures: morning movies downtown, lunch with Mark, an orange lace-trimmed slip from Bonwit Teller. Then I returned to the rubble on my study floor—overdue books, 4-by-6 cards, magic markers, dead ballpoint pens, a Red Sox mug where mold ballooned over stale coffee—and cleared a space for what would blow up to a seven-year episode: "working on my thesis."

*   *   *

Within three years, the Boston architectural firm that had hired Mark was in decline, and he accepted a position just outside Buffalo. Friends commented, "Not Buffalo! Why Buffalo?" Or they asked with point: "You mean there's life west of the Charles?"

We packed our bags, our kids and our timid Great Dane into the station wagon and made for the sunset. We were going to a new land where I would complete my original study of Lezama Lima's *Paradiso* and Mark would conquer the world.

Conquer it he did. Mark began coming home long after we'd finished supper, a stranger who looked as if he'd been at a shoot-out; and he brought the shoot-out with him. It followed him into our bed and crawled into his nightmares. Neither family gatherings at home, nor the children in the car waiting to leave for a weekend in the country, nor even a cozy hotel room in Switzerland was safe from the office phone call. "I've got a lot of mouths to feed," he said to justify his distractions. Or: "When I let someone go, a whole family suffers." Indeed it did.

June 1976: it was Commencement morning. The class of '76 milled around Harvard Yard in crimson robes waiting for ceremonies to begin, but the prospects for an outdoor ceremony grew dim with stormy skies and thunder. We punned on our speaker, the German novelist: *Grass is going to get wet.* The clouds dipped lower, charcoal black, theatrical. We spoke our doubts about the mantra, *It's never rained at a Harvard Commencement.* Standing at the head of the line of dons in colorful robes and gold-tasseled velvet caps, the mayor of Cambridge looked up at the sky with a wince and took the first processional step. As he did, the skies parted and shafts of sunlight illuminated the Yard to a chorus of *Aaahhh's,* laughter, applause.

"This triumphant day"—Harvard University Commencement, 1976

There's no laughter in the photos we took that day. Mark is forcing a smile; my complexion is sallow, and I'm so skinny that my sandaled feet look like tennis racquets. In one photo I'm holding a cigarette, looking tough.

It was an act. Again, I was in a troubled marriage. At bottom, I was afraid I would come up short on selflessness or wisdom or whatever generous impulse keeps other people married *no matter what* so they can spare their children the words no child should hear—"Mom and Dad have decided to separate, but it's not your fault."

Many couples have problems because they don't want to be with each other. I wanted more of Mark and I couldn't get it. These are my cameos of our life together:

He's rowing on Moosehead Lake in Maine, where he's rented a cabin we can't afford. He's brought along wine, a record player, two huge speakers and our favorite record, the soundtrack from *A Man and a Woman*.

He's in our minuscule galley kitchen, stuffing a Thanksgiving goose with prunes he's already stuffed with liver paté, a Julia Child cookbook open on the counter. After dinner he'll carry the dirty dishes into the bathroom, dump them in the bathtub and wash them with baby shampoo.

He's building a hutch for the baby ducklings we've brought back from Vermont. The landlord, dear Mr. Bettencourt, is not amused. "Don't worry," I tell him. "Mark's an architect. He knows what he's doing."

Mark and Carla are kneeling next to the bathtub where the baby ducks are swimming, diving, *beep beep beep*.

He's covered a huge cardboard box with cloth and drawn the face of a clock on it. Now he's pulling it over Carla's head and hanging our kitchen timer around her neck so she ticks when she goes out for Trick-or-Treat.

We're holding hands at the altar and reciting: *For, lo, the winter is past, the rain is over and gone; the flowers appear on the earth;*

the time of the singing of birds is come, and the voice of the turtle is heard in our land.

He's holding me tightly. *All you have to do is follow my rhythm: one-two-swishswish.* And *swishswish* go our ice skates, faster and steadier as we skate arm-in-arm, humming the theme from *Doctor Zhivago.*

We're crying, holding newborn Nathaniel, who's too weak to drink more than an ounce at a feeding even though we use a "preemie" nipple. Nathaniel falls asleep after an ounce or less, and he'll sleep forever if we don't wake him.

I've come home and found his car already in the driveway. An electric joy propels me inside the house; the coast is clear, no children around, and we laugh all the way upstairs to the bedroom.

Weeks before we leave Boston, he's come home from work waving some papers and summoning us into the kitchen. *What is it, what is it?* They're tickets for a *Queen Elizabeth II* cruise, to make us feel better about leaving Boston.

But the *QE2* will not join my cameo collection.

Hispanic Becomes Me

ON BUFFALO'S WEST SIDE, at D'Youville College, I was hired to teach language skills to Spanish-speaking students, mostly Puerto Ricans, who were preparing to be bilingual teachers. It was not quite the future I'd imagined for myself when I was at Harvard, but neither was high-school teaching, and that's what I'd been doing since moving to Buffalo in 1976. No college jobs were to be found, even for a Harvard Ph.D.

Milagros, Miguel, Domingo, María Cristina; the names in my D'Youville student list surprised me. In my first class, the men's *agua de colonia* reminded me of all my important Cuban men: Father, Tío Miguel, Evelio. The women students, meticulously dressed, smelled of brilliantine and flowery perfumes, except for Elsie and Bruni, who were Pentecostals, wore their hair down to the waist and never wore a pair of slacks. Would I like to go to one of their services, they asked, and I accepted.

Inside the dilapidated brick building that had once been a movie house and was now their church, people stood up and threw their arms into the air, crying out, *Aleluya ¡Señor! ¡Señor, Dios mío!* Babies wrapped in blankets slept as soundly as if they'd been in their cribs; or opened their little mouths and ate what mothers fed them out of glass jars. They were the faithful, camping out, waving and calling the Lord's name: *¡Ay, Jesús!* I'd never seen anything like this in Cuba, where we had quietly sat through Mass in a suburban church, every now and then blotting the perspiration that ran down our torsos.

Mari, my youngest student at D'Youville, raised pigeons on her roof and cooked them in broth—*caldo de paloma.* Nilda's uncle raised roosters and took them to illegal cockfights in nearby Dunkirk. Denise's father grew *recao,* a tropical plant unknown to me, in his West Side garden. Otilia, a student's mother, was the queen of vegetable-and-root tamales wrapped in banana leaves; she boiled them inside an oil drum set over a pyre in her Lower West Side backyard. *Pasteles,* the exotic things were called. The students' favorite emblem was the *coquí,* a small frog embroidered on shirts, worn as pendants on gold chains or glued as decals onto cars.

This wasn't Cambridge. It wasn't Havana, either. Was I one of *them?* Was this "home"?

It couldn't be. Their vocabulary was different from mine. *¡Ay, Bendito!*—Oh, Blessed One—was sometimes shortened to *Bendito,* or even *'diiiito.* They changed the meanings of "my" words, calling our *frijoles,* our Cuban black beans, *habichuelas,* which in Cuba meant green beans. Earrings, *aretes,* they called *pantallas,* but in Cuba *pantallas* were screens or lampshades. Some words caused real problems, like *bicho*—"bug" in Cuban—or *concha,* "seashell."

"Ana, you have a little *bicho* on your blouse," I warned a student by the elevator. She opened her eyes wide and whispered, "*Profesora, bicho* is the man's 'thing'."

Fue a la playa a buscar conchas, I wrote on the board: *He went to the beach to look for shells.* Muffled laughter. The women gathered around me after class: "*Profesora, concha* is the woman's 'thing'."

The most amazing verbal phenomenon was the mixing of Spanish and English until the languages ran together. I was witnessing the birth of a dialect:

Standard Spanish	English	New Word
techo	roof	roofo
mercado	market	marqueta
alfombra	carpet	carpeta
cuentas	bills	biles
jardín	yard	yarda
enfermera	nurse	nursa
abrigo	coat	cou
camión	truck	tro

My affection for the students was immediate and reciprocated; but when I returned their examination papers in "Spanish for Native Speakers" class, the Hispanic students noticed that the only two *A's* had gone to non-Hispanics.

"*¡No es justo!* That's unfair!" they protested. "How do you think it makes us feel?"

Their grades had told them that they were less than 100 percent Puerto Rican. Worse, the "Americans" had invaded their linguistic territory and beaten them on home ground.

In the Puerto Rican students, I saw myself. History had branded them just as it had branded me. For them, it had happened in 1898 when Puerto Rico became part of the United States. Back-and-forth migration grew to be part of Puerto Rican life. With it came loss of home culture, weakened family ties, reduced native-language literacy, interrupted schooling, minority status in the continental United States.

Was this my chance to do what I hadn't been able to do for the people in the *bohío?* These Puerto Ricans were my people, too. They'd given me a semblance of home. Listening to their lamentations, I felt that I wouldn't have traded teaching at D'Youville College for a position at Radcliffe or Wellesley or any place of the kind.

Raúl Russi was an older student, a man with a *café con leche* complexion, mustache and sideburns and an easy smile. He limped around the seminar table the first day of class, going from student to student and shaking hands.

Raúl had been the first Puerto Rican police officer in Buffalo's history. He'd been shot while making an arrest, and the bullet had shattered his shinbone. "I could see it shining through my uniform when I was lying there on the curb waiting for the ambulance." Within hours after surgery, his room overflowed with flowers and cards, TV cameramen, elected officials, Hispanics and more Hispanics. All in one night, he'd become a hero as well as a disabled man with a wife and two children to support.

While he was convalescing at home, a stranger called. It was Sister Denise Roche, D'Youville's president. She wanted to know what he was planning to do with his life because she would like him to attend D'Youville College. Raúl told her that he couldn't afford a private college. "How would you like to come to D'Youville for free?"

When I saw Raúl delighting in the Borges short stories we were reading in class, in their ironies and twists of fortune, I understood that his own life had prepared him for Borges. And I imagined how the diffident Argentinean writer might have admired this *gaucho* who, as a boy, had helped his father clean office bathrooms, then had become a police officer, a disabled hero, and finally a student who saw his own life in Borges's constructed labyrinths.

Raúl approached me after class. "So what do you do when you're not teaching?"

"Me? I have my family. I read. I write."

"You ever come down to the West Side?"

"No."

"Ever do anything for the Hispanic community?"

"Sure. I teach Hispanics. You're my students."

"Yeah, but you get paid to do that. What do you do that you don't get paid for?"

"What do you mean?"

Side by side, clipboards in hand, we walked the West Side registering Hispanics to vote. We climbed on wrecked porches; entered houses where sometimes the seat of a car served as the only chair; accepted tiny cups of Bustelo coffee. We explained why it was important to vote and helped people fill out their registration forms. Sometimes I thought I should be home reading instead, but the discarded condoms, liquor bottles and syringes lying along the curbs told me this was where I had to be. As Martí had written: "With the poor of the earth do I cast my destiny."

Soon after meeting, Raúl and I worked on a mission for another Puerto Rican named Raúl. The man was running for city court judge, the first time a Hispanic had done so in Buffalo. Son of a migrant family, Raúl Figueroa had worked next to his father in the tomato fields not far from Buffalo, scrubbing his little green hands with Clorox so other kids at school wouldn't make fun of him. His high-school guidance counselor had urged him to go into vocational training: "You're good with cars and electrical things. You're not really college material." Figueroa ignored the advice, went on to college and law school, and passed the New York State Bar exam on his first try.

That election summer of 1982 turned many Buffalo Hispanics into first-time campaign workers who perfumed the Board of Elections rooms with the scent of *pasteles*, rice-and-pigeon-peas, *pastelillo* meat pies. For a few weeks, Puerto Rican take-out replaced Buffalo chicken wings, and the exotic fragrances drew Board employees to our tables to ask about the food. Terms of endearment went back and forth in Spanish, and I was caught in a downdraft of verbal embraces: "*Mi cielo*—my sky, my sweet—*pass me those registration sheets.*" "*Mi amor*—my love—*is this signature valid?*" "*Mami, check this address.*"

I worked the phone banks on Election Day. One of the people I called asked me to repeat Raúl Figueroa's last name, then asked,

The two Raúls

"He's not a *spic,* is he?" "Yes, he is," I replied, "and I'm one too, and we'd appreciate your vote."

"You got it," the voice on the phone proffered.

That night, Russi and I covered the West Side. He was at the wheel as I held the megaphone. "*¡Salgan a votar por Raúl Figueroa!* Get out there and vote for Figueroa!"

When victory was official, we spilled out of the Delaware Avenue campaign headquarters, perched on the hoods of our cars, opened champagne and drank in silence. I've saved a victory night photo of the "two Raúls." Russi is in a short-sleeved *guayabera* shirt, right index finger up in the air, making a victory speech; while Figueroa, in his dark suit and navy-blue tie embroidered with tiny green buffaloes, is standing with him shoulder to shoulder.

Twenty years after the election, the judge came to my house and fixed my hall-light switch. Then he asked: "What else needs fixing?" His guidance counselor was right about one thing: the man could really do electrical work.

* * *

I'd learned all I needed to learn about being Hispanic. And then a community meeting made me wonder all over again.

The discussion that night—a loud discussion—was about the future of bilingual education in Buffalo. Abruptly, someone behind me yelled: "We're not going to let white people tell us how to educate our children."

Wait a minute.

Papa Karman, sitting on his porch in Havana's swank El Vedado neighborhood, had once rolled up his shirtsleeve and shown me his forearm. "Look, we're white. Don't you forget."

Shame on Grandfather. Shame on history. But how can I say I'm not blanca? *And if I am* blanca, *does that mean I'm not loyal to the cause?*

I turned to Raúl Russi and said: "Listen, I'm white. Are you going to tell me I'm *not* white?"

"Not now," he whispered. "After the meeting."

Later, at the Towne Restaurant, over a bowl of rice pudding, he explained: "You're white, *and* you're not white. Your color is white, but that's only part of it. You're a *latina,* one of us. In that sense, you're not white—not anymore."

My wide-eyed stare made him laugh, and his laughter made me angry.

"Don't be scared," he said. "You're in good company." He picked up the tab and walked me to my car. "Listen. You might *think* you're white, but the world out there doesn't think so."

I was furious at his breezy manner. Instead of going home, I headed for the breakwater at the bottom of Ferry Street so I could cool down. There, by myself, listening to the swift Niagara River, I told Raúl off. *Just because YOU give me a new identity doesn't mean I have one. Who the hell are you to tell me I'm not white?*

I'd come from a different island, a different culture, a different family. I didn't fly to San Juan for Christmas, didn't have an aunt in Ponce waiting to feed me *pernil* and *arroz con habichuelas.*

Cuba had branded me with a singularity that wouldn't go away; it was part of me, a wedge that separated me even from Hispanics. *I'm white but I'm not white. I'm Hispanic but I'm not Hispanic. I'm always "something else."*

Who then am I? What am I?

And then I heard myself answer: *Raúl and the others are your people. He is just giving a name to what you've already become. In Cuba, you were white. Here, you're Hispanic.*

Freedom

I WAS A JIGSAW PUZZLE with Cuban pieces, Hispanic pieces, American pieces. The American pieces of myself I owed to humble epiphanies—moments when affection and geography, place and heart coincided and I yearned for nothing beyond the present time and place.

* * *

(At a gallop in Medina, New York, c.1980)

Spring after spring
those Canada geese
returning home
to fields of wintered corn,
their calls announcing
paradise regained,
had awakened a longing
for the streets of Havana.

This April
Mary saddled up
the tall bay and the gray,
and we rode
into fields of wintered corn
disturbing a flock of geese
who took flight over our heads,
and our horses shied.
We broke into gallop and laughter,
yelled our war cries
full speed the horses
each stride drumming the word
home,
home perhaps,
perhaps home
at last.

*   *   *

Linen napkins in place, my seven-year-old son and I were waiting for our dinner aboard the stern-wheeler *Mississippi Belle,* enjoying the whoosh-whoosh of the paddles, the dense vegetation, the islets and sandbars. "Look, Nathaniel," I pointed at the riverbank—"fishing!" Two teenage boys with fishing poles were sitting close together at the end of a rickety dock. It was right out of *Huck Finn.* The boys were eyeing the *Mississippi Belle,* and just as she glided by, they stood up, turned around and dropped their pants.

How could I explain *mooning* to Nathaniel? *Boys will be boys?* No, that would imply that he too ought to "moon" someday. *That's terrible,* on the other hand, would've spoiled our trip. And yet those four white buttocks, those fleshy headlights beaming into the misty dusk, had precipitated an ethical crisis. Nathaniel was looking at me, waiting for an interpretation. "It's their river,"

I finally said. "They're fishing, and we're scaring the fish away. 'Get off the river,' is what they're telling us with their bottoms. We wouldn't do that, of course."

Inside myself, I thought hard. Had those Americans who'd desecrated the Mighty Mississippi, who'd "mooned" on the shores of the American Ganges, represented the United States in general? Were those buttocks a symbol of U.S. culture? Was this stern-wheeler, paddling on sacred American waters, more Melville than Twain? Were we in the wrong country?

My thoughts turned more and more grave until the counter kicked in. *This* is what the USA is about: freedom pure and simple. Better a "moon" than a tyrant's boot on my son's neck.

An angel in the form of a waitress appeared with a little basket: cornbread and biscuits, honey butter. As we enjoyed our dinner, the real moon rose over the dark treetops and I looked at Nathaniel across the table. *Mooning and all, he'll grow up safe in this imperfect, spectacular country.*

✳   ✳   ✳

Some years earlier, not long after arriving in Buffalo, I had taken off for the open road, getting on the New York Thruway to drive all the way to Houston. It was my first vacation alone, a reward for the plague-like seven years I'd spent poring over Lezama Lima's *Paradiso* and writing a three-hundred-forty-five-page thesis typed on a portable Olivetti flanked by tiny plastic bottles of white-out in different stages of caking. No sooner had I walked into CopyCat at Harvard Square with my completed manuscript than every single copy machine crashed at once. This breakdown might have been Lezama Lima's parting gift to me, a playful example of his bizarre cause-and-effect theory: *A man could—without knowing what he was doing—turn on a light in a room and thereby cause the beginning of a waterfall in Lake Ontario.*

The car trip wasn't just a reward; I was getting away from

Buffalo because I had decided to divorce yet again, and I needed courage. In particular, I needed the company of someone who had known me when I was younger and stronger. A schoolmate, Andrea Barroso, had called from out of the blue. She was teaching at the University of Texas in Houston. Andrea would be the first school friend I'd seen in sixteen years. "I remember everything about Cuba, or at least *cantidad*—a bunch of things," she'd said over the phone. Andrea would remind me of the person I'd been before turning eighteen.

I gunned my husband's Chevy Caprice, a boat of a car upholstered in plush red and loaded with electric windows, an eighttrack tape player for my Helen Reddy—*I am woman, hear me roar*—and cruise control that let me drive with two bare feet up on the dashboard. Truckers honked; I raised a foot in salute and sped on, looking for campgrounds before dusk. When the morning sun illuminated my orange pup tent, I woke up inside a radiant pumpkin.

In Houston, Andrea was waiting with stories, simple stories. Taken one by one, each was pretty modest.

Remember the day we hoisted you onto the tall classroom cabinet and waited for Doctora Varela to start her class?

Remember the afternoon we lifted Doctora Albizuri's Mini-Morris onto the sidewalk and left it there?

Our yearbook voted you "most likely to succeed."

Evelio really, really loved you.

The aggregate was more than enough. Her stories reminded me of a time in my life when I'd had gumption, when I'd shown courage, when I'd been lucky in love. Our friends are the true keepers of our selves—archivists who hold the missing pieces of our jigsaw.

On the trip back to Buffalo I drove hard, twelve hours at the wheel. One evening, after dusk, I was seeing double along the dark highway, praying for a place to eat and sleep. *Mulberry Grove, Indiana,* the sign read. I found an unlit campground where an attendant led me into the dark, pointed to an empty space, told me "no food, nope, camp store's closed," and vanished.

My legs trembled when I stepped out of the car; my wrist gave when I tried to drive the first aluminum stake into dry clay soil. I felt tears coming. Two men approached with a hissing Coleman, a hammer and hefty stakes.

"We'll give you a hand, sure thing," one of them said. "Ain't rained much a'tall." Then came a line straight out of a horror film. "Go on over to that trailer yonder an' we'll get this tent up lickety-split."

They pointed at a pair of dimly lit Stephen King trailers where they might have their way with me and stab me to death. I followed their orders, chastising myself as I walked in the dark. *Why did you keep driving past sunset? Only a girl who's listened to too much Helen Reddy would go camping by herself.*

From inside one of the trailers, two women came forth and handed me a plate: hot dog on a bun, potato salad, an ear of corn and sliced tomato. "Wanna beer?" they asked. I pulled a webbed aluminum chair close to the campfire and heard the men approach, laughing and slapping their thighs. "Hot damn! That dirt out there is *SEE-MENT!*"

The women disappeared into the trailers and re-emerged with fiddles and banjoes. All four of them struck up. The crickets fell silent, and the full moon sank on the horizon, as the musicians began a concert full of riffs and improvisations. They poked fun at each other mid-song: *Don't be showboatin' now, Earl;* and *Pshaw, Loretta,* when Loretta sang, "Oh, I had a little chicken and she wouldn't lay an egg."

I released my death grip on the Budweiser can, sat back and discovered the stars.

I wasn't there, really. I was in a matinee Western featuring two cowboys—or two men in jeans, fancy buckled belts, checkered shirts with mother-of-pearl buttons—and three cowgirls round a campfire, under what might have been but probably weren't cottonwoods. And I recited a brand-new credo: *I believe in the kindness of people in this country, amen.*

"Time to turn in." The men were handing me two folded blankets. "There you go, young lady. Might get chilly. Just leave the blankets by the trailer when you head out tomorrow." And then they were gone, those kind Americans and their Coleman.

* * *

Buffalo, December 5, 1991. They were giving Mozart's *Requiem,* on the 200th anniversary of the composer's death, with a full choir at St. Joseph's Church. It was a cold, blustery night in the middle of the work week. My sofa whispered: *Stay home, bundle up!* Snow was coming down hard. *Snow plus Mozart.* How could I stay home? I'd have Mozart all to myself, because who else would venture out on a night like this?

The bumper-to-bumper traffic began a mile before the church. An accident, I guessed—an early winter fender-bender. Up ahead at the traffic light on the corner of Main and Winspear, a crowd bundled in scarves and heavy coats, mittens and hats, looked like figures in a Breughel portrait. When the light changed, Mozart's faithful rushed to cross. Inside the church, some began to unfurl papers; they'd brought the *Requiem* score. The first notes took my breath away. I knew I belonged with these people. I knew this was my city.

The Flame That Consumes

Late 1996. "COME OUT to the farm and bring the grandchildren. We'll find you a Christmas tree."

Ellie, a good friend, had invited us to her farm a half-hour south of Buffalo. My daughter Carla, her husband Gillian, their four children and I took our places in the station wagon, all of us weather-proofed: thermal underwear, boots, parkas, zip-up snowsuits, hats and mittens. It was a winter-perfect day, snowing just as people in Buffalo talk about snow. "It's really coming down!" "It's blowing and drifting!"

Within half an hour we were out in the field deciphering the tracks in the snow, calling out *rabbit, deer, raccoon, mouse*. Gregory, my eldest grandson, pulled little William's sled along while Nick and Woody, brave scouts, walked ahead looking for our Christmas tree. The adults hung back, watching the boys. "City's no place for kids! Look at them. They love it out here."

Ellie spotted the right tree. We brought it down with hoopla. She crouched, took off her right mitten, counted thirty-six growth rings, counted again sliding her thumbnail carefully from ring to ring. "Thirty-six," she said, turning to me with a smile so soft as to be a purr. "Olga, this is your thirty-sixth winter in the United States, isn't it? I bet this is your family tree!"

Ellie's words, so kind, cut me to the quick. *No,* I reflected silently, *my family tree would be a Cuban tree.*

How real was Cuba in me? So much of my sense of being Cuban seemed sheer faith, a belief in things unseen. Uprooted people must go through life making statements of faith to themselves. Then a thought occurred. *What if I die without going home again? I'm fifty-six years old; it could happen.* "Promise me you'll scatter my ashes over Havana Harbor," I'd once asked my son and daughter. They had called my request "overly dramatic," even while agreeing to it.

On my feet or in an urn, I was going back home.

❊   ❊   ❊

"*¡Boba!* Silly! You're the only one holding out. Havana is full of Europeans, Canadians, Latinos, even Americans."

The U.S. embargo of Cuba and the ban on tourism had been effective barriers against returning; but then my brother Roberto had gone back, saying that the embargo didn't apply to us because Father's cousin Eduardito was alive—albeit barely—in Havana. "We have family there, *chica!* You have a legal right to visit!"

Should I go?

If I don't, I'm going to die without seeing Cuba.

What if they jail me when I return?

Better jail than not going back.

I called Father in Santa Barbara, California, and gave him the news.

"You're going back? What for?" he asked.

I didn't know. Maybe I was a Canada goose returning to its autumn cornfields.

✻   ✻   ✻

*A girl in white is seated on the Malecón seawall, swinging her
legs, playing with the ocean, almost but not quite getting her white
sandals wet. I recognize her dress, the red and blue cross-stitching at
the neckline. Mother made that dress for me.*

*Her hair is braided; her bangs reach her eyebrows. Her brown
eyes, solemn, are fixed on the horizon.*

*The girl in white is aglow, lit up inside. She's a mariner's lan-
tern, signaling: Vuelve. Come back.*

✻   ✻   ✻

Thirty-six years—it's been thirty-six years.

The five-week wait for the flight to Havana was interminable.

My house in Miramar was resonating—a two-story cello humming the music of my spheres.

I could hear it plainly.

✻   ✻   ✻

I started behaving like a tourist, leafing through guidebooks
of Havana, the city where I was born. Oblivious to the aisle traffic at The Village Green Bookstore on Elmwood Avenue, I slid
down to the carpeted floor with a copy of *Havana: Portrait of a
City*, my fingertips feeling the illustrations almost as a blind
person's fingers read Braille.

For decades, American bookstores had expunged Cuba from
their shelves. Whenever I looked for Cuba, the titles would leap-
frog from Chile or Croatia to Cyprus or Czechoslovakia. But
now books in full color, guidebooks with maps, were for sale.
You could see the stonework on the porticoes: fanning scallop
shells, twining vines, roses widening open with abandon, a display of tropical stone made supple as ribbon-candy.

What did I know about all this back then? Our high-school

field trips to the Old City, *La Habana Vieja*, were wasted on young girls who complained about the heat, about having to get off the bus and go into some boring old building.

I could tell the sun was due west when the Malecón facades in that book had been photographed. The shimmering light that fell on robin's-egg blue, lemon yellow and shades of rose had made the stone structures levitate, as if the ocean had jumped the seawall and turned the buildings into floating islands.

Home is wasted on those who think it's theirs forever.

*   *   *

It was as if I were already in Havana. Old Cuban sayings and songs went swarming in my head—like a 1950's jingle for Colgate announcing the toothpaste that beautifies your teeth and perfumes your breath: *Colgate limpia y embellece los dientes y le perfuma el aliento.*

Just then I got word that Father, eighty-nine years old, had taken a fall in a supermarket parking lot in Santa Barbara. A shopper had found him on the asphalt, unconscious. He had a concussion; his condition was grave.

I was not ready to do without Father's gentleness, his voice calling me *Olguita.* My busy stream of language became a single sentence: *I don't want him to die.*

During the flight to California, I looked down at the snow-covered Rockies and wondered why we were going west instead of south. *I've boarded the wrong flight. I want to get out.*

*   *   *

Father's face was a patchwork of purple and scabs, his arms black-and-blue. He was dazed, and didn't see me. Better that way for now; better he didn't see me seeing him like this.

*   *   *

Although my brother Roberto also lived in Santa Barbara, I stayed at Father's apartment on Salsipuedes Street, where his presence—and even Mother's so many years after her death—was strong. *Sal si puedes:* get out if you can. When Roberto had found them an apartment there twenty years before, Mother and Father had made light of the street-name, but we knew it contained a meaning. They would not get out of there alive. They would not see Cuba again.

Instead, they'd brought Cuba to Salsipuedes Street: framed prints of a sugar mill at work, a photo of the Malecón with the Morro Castle in the distance, our patron saint the *Virgen de la Caridad* above the desk piled with Medicare forms, cancelled checks, receipts and newspaper clippings. Inside Father's desk drawer was the 1960 church calendar that my grandmother, Mama Angélica, had marked up so we'd always remember family saint's days, birthdays, death dates. On Mother's night table was a sepia photo of Father, handsome, under sail on his star-class boat *Ciclón,* stopwatch in hand, eyes on the sails. Under Father's bed was a shoebox filled with three years' worth of letters he'd written Mother after she'd left Cuba in 1964. Among these objects, the feeling of exile was close and palpable.

I saw he'd kept Mother's straw sewing bag although she'd been gone for seven years. The vivid purple, turquoise and magenta had faded, as if the bag had also expired. And yet it brought Mother back to life and into the room with me. It held the things she'd once touched, the red pincushion she'd called *el tomate,* her bobbins, rickrack, tailor's chalk and gold thimble. Already an old woman, mother had made herself into a seamstress. In Dallas, their first home together in the United States, I watched her kneel in front of a client and mark a hem. Now in my hand was Mother's very own business card: *Alterations Elsa Terry de Karman.* "The real money is in alterations," she once observed.

Under the sewing notions were her dressmaker's notebook, a compendium of sewing secrets, fabric inventories and "helpful hints" written in a steady hand:

— Jerseys that run, put running part in bottom of hem, bottom of jacket & sleeves.

— For top stitching 2 bobbins one on top of the other. Needle #14.

— Hong Kong facing for jacket hems, bias strip.

How painstaking Mother was, how disciplined and persevering. In these notes, I could see her telling me to do as she had done: refine, make things with care.

Here was a marbled notebook I'd seen before:

My Cook Book—Elsa Terry de Karman
first started in Miramar, Cuba 1943
continued in Dallas Texas 1967
" " " in Santa Barbara CA 1975

It had eighty numbered pages beginning with a table of contents, an alphabetical index, the name of a cake or soup, soufflé or marmalade followed by the name of whoever had given her the recipe—family member, Havana neighbor or new American friend. "Four-Alarm Texan BBQ *Ida Mae*" coexisted with "Guava Empanadas *Carmelina Solís*," "Yam Desert Boniatillo *Alicia Diago*." In her Santa Barbara kitchenette I saw her assembling spices and greens, testing a recipe she'd learned in adult education. Mother was a magician; she invented new lives for herself and wove them into the old one.

*   *   *

I began to dismantle the apartment. Father wasn't going to live. He wasn't coming back here. I gathered up the family pictures: six generations scattered through a bedroom. Great-great-grandmother Teodosia Basden de Terry's hand-painted miniature was well over a hundred years old. Mama Angélica was still young in one that caught her holding an open parasol. I found Papa

Karman in his tuxedo, the one Mother transformed into my traveling suit. Three huge women, dead serious, up to their necks in black satin—Minina, Adelaida and Antonia Terry—were Mother's grandmother and grand-aunts. A footnote to the photograph read *Cienfuegos, Cuba, mid 1800's.* I was about twelve years old in a photo that Tío Miguel took of me at the farm, holding a tube of Prell in one hand and the garden hose in the other. Sultán was next to me, tethered to the guava tree. Right next to it, as if to play with time, Mother had placed a color photo—the only one in the room—of my grandson Gregory; he was throwing autumn leaves up into a very blue Buffalo sky.

Everything in the apartment counted. All of it would give me strength when I'd be in Cuba by myself.

Cuba? Am I still going? What about Father?

I recognized a bold Marimekko print covering another book.

"Santa Barbara, June 10, 1983—My daughter Olga gave me this beautiful notebook for my 80th birthday with the request that I write my memoirs. Never having written anything in my life, I hardly know where to begin. And why? Is her curiosity inherited from me? I used to question my grandmother Tatá endlessly and she would finish by saying, 'If you ask me anything more I won't continue.' But it was fascinating for me to learn what her life had been like in Cienfuegos where she was born but never returned, always saying, 'That's where the devil screamed three screams, and no one heard him.' "

✳   ✳   ✳

All I had known about Mother's ancestors would have fit inside her gold thimble. Now, reading the pages she'd left, I learned that the Terry fortune had come from railroads and from a sugar mill they'd inhabited since the 1820's. Mother's grandmother Tatá, it said there, set free the slave she'd been given as a wedding present. Our branch of the Terry family—Mother's grandparents,

*Mama Angélica as a young
woman with her parasol*

The Terry women

Antonio Terry and Antonia Latté (Tatá), and a child I'd never heard of—had fled Cienfuegos at the end of the 19th century:

"Antonio [Mother's grandfather], just returned after two years in France, was full of republican ideas so he joined a group of plotters against the Spanish regime. Soon their plotting was discovered, but a friendly Spaniard in the government came and warned the family that their house was about to be burned. As they lived with Antonio's parents, they, grandpa & grandma and a new born baby, Lily, got in a sailboat and made for New Orleans. They left behind everything they owned, but they were able to take a trunk full of gold. When they started bringing the trunk up the stairs of the hotel in New Orleans, there were no elevators then, it was too much to carry, the trunk fell down and burst open and a rain of gold coins showered the lobby."

* * *

After New Orleans they moved to Philadelphia, where Antonio studied medicine. Now that he was far from the family fortune, he had to make a living; and his years in Paris hadn't prepared him for the real world. Mother's father, my Papa Juan, was born in Philadelphia. By the time Mother herself was born, the family was in New York City. "One thing stands out from those years," Mother noted, "and that is Papa taking us all up on the roof to look at Halley's Comet."

In 1917, Mother's parents were divorced. Her sister Consuelo stayed in New York with my grandmother Olga, while Mother, Papa Juan and my great-grandmother Tatá came to Cuba. "As our ship got to the mouth of Havana harbor," Mother recorded, "I saw the work that was going on to raise the U.S. battleship *Maine*."

Papa Juan and Tatá rented an old mansion on Avenida General Lee. Mother found slave manacles and leg irons in the carriage house and ran with them to Tatá, who had a bonfire lit and threw the irons into the flames. The house had formal gardens, hold-cages where the cook kept her chickens, a summer dining room linked to the house by a corridor "so long that Papa and I used it as a shooting gallery," and a salon for parties:

"The most fun was when Papa led the guests in a dance called the Paul Jones—or the *poyón*, as they pronounced it. In Cuban, that also means 'fat chicken.' The room had forty couples and it was not even crowded."

Mother adored listening to her grandmother's stories. "I used to stand by Tatá's rocking chair and comb her silky snow-white hair. Those were the moments she would take to reminisce; about her youth and marriage in Cienfuegos, the family's flight and exile in the United States, and later Paris and Spain. To this day I can still think of many things I would have liked to ask. How I wish she had kept a diary or a book of memoirs."

✳   ✳   ✳

I spent mornings and afternoons at Cottage Hospital and evenings at Salsipuedes Street, bagging Father's things for Goodwill and setting aside what would go to my brother and to me. I kept Father's sailing album and the faded business card that read *Casa Karman, O'Reilly 519;* his Cuban passport, last stamped in 1967; and a well-worn Dallas street map with his route to work highlighted in yellow.

Bitter memory, that one—Father's defeat. He'd come to Dallas because a Texan who'd been Casa Karman's supplier of American-made radios had promised him a job. When Father arrived at age sixty, the Texan put him to work assembling radios in a Quonset hut without air-conditioning. But Mother was practical; she gave the boss a bottle of El Baturro Spanish cider at Christmas. Soon they were able to buy a used Mercury so that Father wouldn't have to take the bus to work.

His adult-education steno pads told a story of sorts. One of them, labeled *Latin* and dated September 1980, contained grammar and quotations from Catullus, Cicero and Horace in spidery handwriting. He was seventy-three years old when he translated the sentence *Horas non numero nisi serenas.* "I count only the happy hours."

In another pad, labeled *French,* I found a line wherein he said he could send only a few Christmas cards—"*Je serai très limité à expedir des cartes*"—because the postal rate had increased.

Why hadn't they told me they had so little? Why hadn't I ever looked in their closets and seen that Mother didn't own a single dress? I could've helped. I didn't know. They were too proud—proud of their old car, their apartment, their adult-education classes, proud of how well they were managing when they walked the aisles at Thrifty's clutching their discount coupons.

Silence is part of exile. Both became daunting as I stood amid their meager possessions. And then a folded piece of paper dropped to the floor:

"FINAL EXIT: Let me die before I wake. Seconal 40 lethal dose with liquor. Valium 500 mg with alcohol. Digitalis—maybe 1 large dose (cardiac) digitalis glycoside."

This too I would keep: the proof that Father chose to persevere even as he'd known all along how to end his life.

❊   ❊   ❊

Could be hours, the doctor said, could be weeks. I pulled the light blanket up to Father's chin and moistened his lips with a wet sponge, then a little Vaseline.

Should I stay with Father or go to Cuba? The choice was so hard I couldn't think it through. I decided to wait for a sign, a voice, a vision or command—something I couldn't ignore.

I'd wheeled him out to the hospital courtyard so that he could enjoy the Santa Inez Mountains and the scent of the eucalyptus trees. He raised his index finger and motioned me to pirouette, show off my dress. *Muy bonita,* he said, *muy bonita mi Olguita.*

He closed his eyes, holding on to a faint smile. Then the voice I'd been awaiting started to speak; but rather than to me, it spoke to Father.

You will be with me in Havana. We'll walk O'Reilly Street, and you'll tell me to be careful with the traffic. You'll protect me. Soon, Papi—soon we're going home.

* * *

Back in Buffalo, I called the convalescent home. The nurse walked to Father's bedside and handed him the phone. "Mr. Karman, Mr. Karman, it's your daughter."

"Hola, Papi. Soy yo, Olguita, Papi."

He answered only with his breathing, and then the sound of the receiver against the sheets.

* * *

Ten days left—ten days and I'll be in Cuba.

Christmas dinner became my *adiós* to Nathaniel, Carla and Gillian and my four grandsons—a dozen Christmas tapers illuminating their dear faces at the dinner table.

This is my family. I've spun them out of my own silk, far from Cuba, in unreal American time. And yet in this unreal time I've become almost old.

"How does it feel to be going back to Cuba, Ma?"

I'm frightened. I don't know anyone there anymore. I'm deserting Papi.

"Wonderful," I said, and began to tell them—for the first time, I realized—about Christmas in Cuba. After the first few sentences I stepped out of myself, and as I listened to my description I realized it must sound like make-believe. If you never saw Christmas at Rinconcito or the pig swinging over the pit, how else could it sound?

✳   ✳   ✳

No matter how far from the farmhouse José went to do the butchering, I could hear the pig's death squeals. José hosed it down, scrubbed the skin with boiling water, split it open and gutted it while we mashed heads of garlic, herbs and spices with mortar and pestle. Right on the kitchen table, we squeezed bitter oranges into the open pig until we had pools of juice in its concavities; then we dug into the mortar for garlic and herbs to rub all over the fresh-smelling flesh. We wrapped the animal in banana leaves and left it marinating until next morning, when it would lie on a filigreed wrought-iron headboard and cook over a bed of coals. First we browned one side. Then the adults, already woozy from too many *mojitos,* flipped it over, they themselves nearly falling into the pit. *¡Ay, Dios mío, cuidado!* My God! Careful, Miguel!

The kitchen was a hive. Even the men wore aprons. My brother and I weren't allowed inside although we could watch Lucía through the open window, an unfiltered Partagás dangling from her lips. She fried plantains, squashed them flat between two layers of paper bags and set them aside to fry again at the last minute: "fisticuffed" plantains, *plátanos a puñetazos.* Black beans simmered; a mound of avocados and pineapples waited for Tía Consuelo to peel and slice for salad; cassava boiled, the *mojo* sauce—olive oil, lime juice and garlic—simmered. Café Pilón was at the ready inside the flannel colander; the lattice-top guava pies oozed deep red.

My brother and I ran to the table when we heard the cry *¡a comer!,* hoping there'd still be empty *taburete* chairs for us. We liked to pick at the cow fur while we ate. After lunch—*the hour of lethargy,* Tío Miguel called it—my brother and I raced each other to the Yucatán hammock for siesta. In the intense heat, Miguel snored while cicadas blasted and not a leaf stirred. Mother and Father napped in the guest room, and on the porch Tía Consuelo sat in her striped canvas chair reading *Bohemia* until her eyes, blue as the Morning Glory blossoms that framed her bedroom window, closed.

Rinconcito, "Little Corner," was at 20 acres a small farm but a land of plenty. Near the house, lettuce and radish grew under mosquito netting; just beyond, a patch of maize was enough to feed three horses and two cows. Then came a patch of sugar cane, some cassava, two lime trees, mango, avocado, guava, Tía Consuelo's hibiscus and jasmine.

At dusk, the sky over Rinconcito turned magenta, orange and gold, with hints of black; peace descended on us then as we took turns watering the four rows of vegetables in their dark raised beds. The farm and the evening stretched far beyond what our eyes could see. My palomino Sultán, grazing just beyond the skeleton of the barn that last year's cyclone had devastated, was finer than Trigger or Silver; and Ferdinando, the black-and-white calf who licked salt out of my hand, felt as if he'd been dipped in wax just for me.

With the last light of the sun, Tío Miguel lit Coleman lamps whose miraculous gauze centers burned without being consumed. A decade or more later, when I read what St. John of the Cross had said about God's love, I remembered those Coleman lamps: *the love of God is a flame that consumes without giving pain.*

After dinner, out came the dominoes, the *centavos* for betting, the toffees wrapped in foil. From the Yucatán hammock where I slept at the farm, I heard dominoes banging against the wood table, Colemans exhaling haaaaaaaaa, my family's playful voices, someone striking a match to light up a Partagás, and mice galloping across the wooden beams above—straight into my dreams.

Dawn and solitude; the adults were still sleeping. After banging my sneakers on the floor to empty them of beetles and spiders and maybe even a scorpion, I laced them up and tiptoed into the new light, the grass still sown with dewdrops and wet webs. I walked to the windowless hut on stilts where we kept grain and saddles, climbed in and inhaled the scent of leather and damp saddle pads, liniment, molasses. When my eyes adjusted to the dark I saw the burlap bags wide open, their edges rolled down as if offering their treasury of grain, and I plunged my bare arms and hands into the pools of seed. It was as if every grain had recognized me and made room. The sweet-feed, sugary and dark, was clinging to me. I whispered the names of the grains: *avena* to the smooth-hulled oats, and *maíz* to the hard corn kernels that touched me with their scratchy nubs, their bits of cob.

Above me, saddles gleamed astride a pole-beam; the butterfly-shaped pads were flecked with gold, chestnut and black. I stood up and brought my face to horsehair and leather and felt my knees give when I inhaled.

Niña, niña el desayuno. I came out when Lucía called me to breakfast. Tía Consuelo and Tío Miguel were already at the table helping themselves to *café con leche* and big buttered crackers, passing the dented sugar bowl, asking their habitual questions, *how did you sleep,* answering with small, almost unnecessary words, and I felt my love for them spill over like an avalanche of grain.

✣ ✣ ✣

In my foyer, scarves, coats, mittens and boots went on; my family was ready to take off into the Christmas night. I kissed them all and closed the door, one foot in Buffalo, the other in Havana.

PART II

Confidence

I'M IRONING THIS SKIRT to take to Cuba.
Estoy planchando esta saya para llevarla a Cuba.
I'm going to walk all over Havana in these sandals.
Voy a caminar por toda La Habana con estas sandalias.
I'm going to see my house again.
Voy a ver mi casa otra vez.
Everything will turn out just fine. You'll see.
Todo te va a salir bien. Tú vas a ver.

✻   ✻   ✻

Snowing in Buffalo.

A girl dressed in white goes skipping ahead of me along the Old City, *La Habana Vieja.* When she turns around, I see red hearts embroidered all around the neckline of her dress. *Follow me,* she indicates.

I go with her into a labyrinth. It's my own city in ruins—

shabby streets, mold-stained walls, tumbledown buildings. I know I am in hell. Farther and farther along the girl skips, until she vanishes.

Wandering on, I read street-names: *Ánimas*/Souls, *Refugio*/Refuge, *Misericordia*/Mercy, *Sol*/Sun, *Amistad*/Friendship, *Luz*/Light, *Aguacate*/Avocado, *Porvenir*/Future.

How can this be hell?

I'm awake. My flight leaves Toronto for Havana this afternoon.

* * *

I won't look down. I'm too scared.
No, I'm going to look.
Where is it?
Where's Havana?
I don't see it.
All I can see are dark blotches, a few faint lights; fireflies.
Where are the lights? It's dark.
Havana, my city of lights, has gone dim.
Someone turned off the lights.

* * *

Then came the dark tarmac, the walk into the congested Arrivals area and the approach to the angel of immigration, guarding the gate to Paradise. The *señorita* looked through my papers.

"Where is your visa, *señora*? We can't let anyone in without a visa. You don't have a visa."

¿Señora? What do you mean señora? *I'm just a teenager!*

She fanned the pages of my passport and returned it even as I showed her my scrap of paper: "*Mire.* Here's my visa number. Someone's waiting for me with my paper visa."

She took no notice of it and said with theatrical disdain: "That's just a number, *señora*. A number is not a visa. Sit over there at the end of the queue."

I'm just a gusana, *a worm who's turned into a tourist.*

Passengers coming in from the tarmac stumbled into me and grabbed whatever they could to steady themselves—my arm, my blouse. Minutes later, over the loudspeaker, a voice called my name, telling me to proceed to the information booth. But the *señorita* was gloating.

"No, *señora.* I can't let you through to *Información.* You don't have a visa."

"But they just called me. My visa is in *Información.*"

"You can't go to *Información* without a visa. Next!"

I was holding up the line, and those behind me quickly grew impatient. The French passengers cursed in French, while the Spaniards told me, in their sociable manner, to go fuck myself. In time, everyone had gotten out the sliding glass doors: Germans, Mexicans, Italians, Spaniards, Canadians, even the old New Jersey Cuban I'd met at Toronto airport. The only one left with me was a young American passenger hollering for his rights. By midnight the young American too had left, and I was alone under the fluorescent lights.

This is home? This is where I'm going to piece myself together?

A guard in olive green took his post at the door. I'd forgotten the olive green; but rather than anger or fear, what overcame me was a sense of my own innocence.

"*Joven,*" I called out to the guard, "young man, watch over me. I'm going to sleep. Don't let anything happen to me."

He looked me over and said, "Don't worry."

I took two T-shirts out of my suitcase, made a blindfold and a pillow and lay down across four plastic chairs. *No harm will come to me in Cuba.* And I dropped like a coin into a transparent ocean, all the way down to a bed of white sand, where I rested until dawn.

✻ ✻ ✻

At first light, two security guards walked in, glanced at me, said good-morning, walked away, returned, pulled up two chairs and began to question me at a whisper: "Life in New York, in *el norte,* what's it like?"

Iván, *good Russian name,* called me *compañera,* a post-revolutionary form of address that implied camaraderie. *"Compañera,* how much do they pay you per day in the United States?"

Instead of the dollar amount, I told them how I lived with my salary. "I pay for my house and my car, clothes, food, dinner at a restaurant now and then, movies, gifts for my family. I travel almost every year. How much do teachers get paid here?"

They discussed their friends' salaries: "More or less 230 pesos a month." That was just under twelve dollars, less than a third of what I was making in Havana in 1958, when I was eighteen years old and teaching English at Colegio Baldor.

"Olga, they say the government over there puts up signs outside the houses of persons who have AIDS."

"Signs?"

"Signs that say: 'Here lives a person with AIDS.'"

I told them: No! We respect human rights. I presented the extreme case of an American prison inmate whose story I'd read. He sued the U.S. government because his magazine subscriptions were being delivered to him late.

"Lies, Olga. You're lying."

"No. I'm serious. I give you my word. *Palabra.*"

They looked at each other, then looked away. In that almost furtive exchange of glances I could see despondency and bitterness, as if my dollop of information had confirmed the existence of a world that brought their own lives into harsh focus.

*   *   *

By mid-morning I was close to tears when the guards told me I could go upstairs to the cafeteria and the bathroom. That first *café con leche* blotted out the feeling that someone was rubbing broken glass against my pupils.

The ladies' room attendant handed me two pieces of toilet paper. When I was ready to leave she stopped me: "I have a daughter in *el norte*. She left five years ago. Do you know a place called Hoboken?"

She wanted me to reassure her, and I did. "Hoboken is nice; your daughter must be happy in Hoboken."

The guards were waiting for me. To pass the time, I told them Buffalo stories. First was the blizzard of '77, the tank-like vehicles going up and down Delaware Avenue shooting hundreds of little flames into the ice on the street. Then came the Buffalo Bills, the day we almost won the Super Bowl except we missed the field goal. I described Niagara Falls, the water vapor "plume" we can see from miles away, and the ice fishing on Lake Erie.

When Iván had had enough of my stories, he blurted out: "Did you pay for your night at the hotel? Demand a refund!"

By their noontime rounds they were just passing me by with a shaking of their heads. It seemed they'd given up on me; or perhaps they were angry at me for not doing anything about my predicament. On one of those sweeps, I asked them what I should do. "Go back to Toronto!" they said.

No, it can't be true! Thirty-six years aching for home, and now this?

"When is the next flight to Toronto?"

"In two days."

Inexplicably, we looked at each other and burst out laughing. I made a fist and banged it on my suitcase. "That's it! I'm staying!"

We laughed at life, at fate, at the Absurd that ruled over them and me. We laughed because we were Cubans, and that's how Cubans have always survived. *We're in this together,* **compañeros!**

* * *

By lunchtime, the airport and the sidewalk outside were again busy with passengers. People walking by the terminal couldn't see in, but I could see them; the glass wall separating us was a one-way mirror.

A young woman, looking about my age when I left Cuba, came up to the glass, checked the fit of her tight skirt, gave it a tug, applied lipstick. Something about her earnestness made me love her and long to be with her. Whoever she was, I had missed her terribly for thirty-six years. For the first time, my eyes welled up, and I knew I was home.

* * *

A man whisked by me, stopped, turned around, looked me up and down, kept going at a clip, then stopped and motioned me to Immigration.

"*¡Aquí estoy!* Here I am!" he pronounced. "I'm Rusty. Here's your temporary visa. It's good for today."

He was about to run off, but *not so fast:* "Temporary? What do you mean 'temporary,' Rusty?" My own authority surprised me. *One night in Havana and I have my Cuban self-confidence back.* "Rusty, listen to me. I've been here sixteen hours. When are you giving me the real visa?"

He, the master of evasiveness: "Later. I'll bring it in person."

"No, no, no," I hammered. "Later nothing—*Nada de eso.* What time *exactly?* Before five or after five?"

"*A las cinco en punto,*" he said—Five on the dot. I didn't believe him.

My two *compañeros* had been eavesdropping and looking into space as if to say *we are not involved with this.* They'd gone as far as they could go—had brought me hot coffee in a tiny paper cup, given me a piece of hard candy, a cigarette I was tempted to light up, a pocket calendar. "Is this for me to keep track of my days inside the airport?" I'd asked.

Their generosity and my temporary poverty had humbled me.

All I'd owned for sixteen hours had been a small suitcase on wheels and family photos I'd passed around. I had been stripped down. I'd had no rights, no recourse. They'd taken me in. They'd welcomed me home.

❖ ❖ ❖

Like faithful bodyguards they stood next to me while I waited for a taxi, but as the car pulled away they walked into the airport without looking back. In their slow gait and bowed heads I thought I saw defeat and hoped I was wrong, hoped it was my own exhaustion I saw.

I was seeing home from the back seat of a Russian Lada: the Malecón Boulevard, the Morro Castle. I looked away just in time to avoid seeing La Punta, the place where Mother, Father and Mama Angélica had waved goodbye to me with their handkerchiefs in 1960. *I'm never going there again.*

A feeling of disbelief overwhelmed all else. *I'm in Havana.* I was numb.

❖ ❖ ❖

Almost no traffic—so unlike back then, and yet the few cars going by were 1950's models, so that every De Soto and every Studebaker fooled me into thinking it's *back then* all over again. Time in Cuba, it seemed, had stood still; it was as if Havana had frozen up in 1960 and was just waiting for me to return. I remembered Borges's short story "The Secret Miracle," where time stands still for a prisoner facing a firing squad and allows him to relive his entire life. The executioners' guns go off when he's done remembering.

Forget Borges. Look! There goes a Morris Minor. And my two-tone '55 Chevy. Follow that car! Nothing has changed. But if nothing has changed, why do I need a visa to be home? Rusty! Stay focused. Call Rusty. If he forgets you, you'll be in Cuba without papers.

I placed the call as soon as I was in my hotel room.

"*Oigo*," a voice answered, and I was on full alert. A government office doesn't answer *oigo*.

"Is Rusty there?"

"Rusty? There's no Rusty here."

I knew it.

"Listen to me. *Óigame.* Did you hear about a lady stuck in the airport for sixteen hours? Well, that's me. I'm exhausted. Please, put Rusty on. I'm not a girl anymore; I'm fifty-six years old. I'm falling-down tired."

Then the last straw: "Naahh. You're not fifty-six years old! Lies. *Mentiras.* You have a young woman's voice. *Voz de jovencita.* Such a pretty voice. Tell me the truth. How old are you?"

Is he taunting or flirting? I wasn't sure, but I was hurting with exhaustion. All I wanted to know was whether Rusty worked there or not. I shifted strategy and played the swooning lady to his gallant.

"*Ay, por favoooor,*" I implored in a syrupy voice. "How can I start my vacation in Cuba with all this worry and uncertainty? How can I go to the beach, nervous like this?"

Lightning-quick the answer: "Hang on…. Rusty will be there at five o'clock sharp. He'll call your room. Don't worry. He'll be there."

All at once my giddiness was upon me. Again I was a daring teenager, wanting to push limits and live off the rush of the dare and the double-dare. Again I was wild.

I'll head straight for the downstairs bar, sit next to the glass case full of cigar boxes, perch on a stool, and plunge into rum, lime, tobacco aroma. Remember, Olguita, a tobacco leaf feels alive, feels like skin to the touch. *I'll order a daiquiri, pretend I'm Ava Gardner—she stayed here once. All the props are in place: al fresco bar, sultry air off the ocean, the notes of a soulful* bolero, *ice cubes going clink clink when someone shakes a glass, clink clink clink the* Guadalupe *remember clink clink clink. I'll be wearing tight white linen, red stiletto-heeled sandals, red nail polish. A handsome man in a* guayabera *will walk in, catch a glimpse of me, sit on the barstool next to mine.*

Un momento. *Who's imagining this scene? What white linen dress? What stiletto heels and red nail polish? Is that me? Have I become a Hollywood* cubana? *Or an* americana *who finds herself exotic in the tropics? If Fidel could read my thoughts he'd say I have a colonized mind. He'd speak for hours about colonization, beginning with Columbus and ending with me.*

Hey! Psssst. Stop daydreaming. Open your eyes. Look out the window, chica. ¡Mira!

The Impervious Melody

THERE'S SOMETHING TENDER about the ocean breeze blowing out the hotel-room curtains. My skin is a lung inhaling, exhaling. *Our Father who art in heaven, give us this day our daily sea.* Five floors below are almond blossoms and tiled terraces. Ocean, light and shadow are playing on each beloved surface.

Lean against the window sill. Surrender. Let the salt air, like a mother cat, lick your kitten face.

All parts of Havana are breathing in unison; I feel the body's pulse. My own body loosens as if someone had untied a bow that was holding it too tightly. *Ego te absolvo,* God whispers in Latin— "I forgive all your trespasses." From fifty years away, a girl's voice is calling: *¡Sal a jugar! ¡Apúrate!* Come out and play! Hurry up!

* * *

The route to Mama Angélica's house is so familiar that I think I'm a homing pigeon flying back to my roosting box at Calle M

#162. Father and I had lunch at M #162 every day the summer I worked for him at Casa Karman.

Back then: I know Mama Angélica listens for the wrought-iron gate just after midday because Father has barely swung it open when she comes rushing out the door in her dark dress and medium-heeled black shoes, applauding and spreading open her arms for a quick *abrazo.* No time for more: Papa Karman, white shirt rolled up once or twice at the cuffs, is at the table ready to be served. Napkin rings, toothpick holders and water goblets are waiting for us on white cloth, exactly where they were yesterday and where we suppose they will always be.

Alo, alo, Papa Karman welcomes us in his native French. I offer my hand so he can press it against his cheek and hold it there for a few seconds. Isaura brings out the soup tureen: *patas con garbanzos,* pigs' feet with chickpeas. Papa Karman is lit up with joy, while Father-the-ascetic sings a different tune: "Too much food, too much." Papa Karman quickly dispatches the diet plate that the cardiologist has prescribed for him. Then, as Father looks the other way, Papa moves on to the regular lunch, because, *voyez,* a man cannot live on boiled fish and grass, no matter what some doctor says. The dessert is guava shells, guava marmalade or guava paste—*give us this day our daily guava*—then black coffee with a gulp of water, and Isaura in bedroom slippers clears the table while we begin our family siesta.

Father lies down on the chaise lounge, unfolds a handkerchief and drapes it over his face. Papa Karman takes his *Paris Match* to the terrace and dozes off with Charles de Gaulle waving at him from an open car on the Champs-Elysées. Mama Angélica and I close the bedroom shutters and take our places on her mahogany bed, dimpling the rose-colored bedspread with our shoes.

Mama Angélica holds my hand and talks about Papa Karman when he was young and fresh in Cuba, "a land of opportunity," at the beginning of the 20th century; she tells me how he took her hand and promised they would never go back to France. Then, in a whisper, she implores: "Turn the radio down just a bit, my sweet." On Radio Kramer, it's Nat King Cole in "Tenderly" or Elvis in "Treat Me Like a Fool," or some girls' group in "Hey-La, Hey-La, My Boyfriend's Back."

Pretending to be asleep, I peek at Mama Angélica, her little hands folded just so, the wisps of black hair wound tightly around the horsehair rolls that are the style for women of her age. She sighs and sleeps under the picture of a young Christ who watches over us and points an index finger at his own flaming heart. Mama Angélica is a geisha dreaming. Her chest rises and falls, plump as a dove, small as a child's pillow.

That was then. Now is now. I'm on foot to Mama Angélica's house, the scent of the ocean as pervasive as on the deck of a sailboat. How simple this is. Over to the right is Tío Miguel's apartment; just ahead on Línea is Tía María's white house; to the right and left are the *grandes dames*, El Vedado's old mansions. But what's happened to them? They are disfigured, pockmarked, with chunks of plaster collapsed on destitute flower beds. Metal rods are sticking out of cracked walls; electrical wires dangle in space. Porches are propped up with wood planks; mounds of rubble rise beneath cracked balustrades. Where have the staircases gone?

Don't look. Don't stare. These people standing around live here. If they see you staring, they'll see their ruins with fresh eyes and they'll know. Breathe. Run. Don't stop again. Run all the way to #162.

Which one is it? All the houses have turned the same dull gray, huddled together like frightened ghosts set upon by sun and sea. *No, tell it like it is. They have been set upon by the Revolution.* But this one here, this iron gate, I recognize; the porch with Moorish tiles, some broken, others missing. This is the one.

Who are those three people on the porch? The rocking chairs are missing; the flowerbeds are gone to weed; the gate is rusted brown.

Papa Karman

Olga and Mama Angélica

Two very serious women and a man stare at me. One of the women, dressed in white from kerchief to cracked patent-leather shoes, whispers something to the others and rushes out through the gate, almost hitting into me as she hurries by. The others glare.

"My grandmother lived in this house," I call out. "Her name was Angélica. Angélica!"

They don't reply. Maybe they think I've come to take the house back. Okay, let's try again. "How pretty everything looks!" And again nothing happens.

I place my hand on the latch and stand still. The man looks at my hand as if he wants to peel it off but I don't move it, not even when he gets up and heads right for me. *Are you coming to give me a shove? Go ahead. I'm not budging.*

He unlatches the gate. "We're the ones who buried your grandmother. We took care of her until the very end. *Pase*—Please come in."

Tell me everything about Mama Angélica. What did she talk about when she got really old? Do you have anything of hers? The sandalwood fan? A handkerchief? Anything? You gave it all to the church? Oh. Could I see her room? We used to take siesta listening to Elvis Presley. Do you remember Elvis?

I feel foolish for mentioning Elvis, but I'm at a loss with these dour strangers who at long last walk me into the dark house, the woman saying her name is Yeyé.

Where has the furniture gone? M #162 is empty of all but the people living inside it. Gone is the glass-top vanity that Mama Angélica let me polish with crumpled-up newsprint and cologne when I was still in braids. Gone from her bedroom is the picture of the young Christ. In its place is something I can't quite make out.

"My altar to Changó," Yeyé explains, waiting for me to react to the name of the African deity.

There stands Changó amid a slew of objects: a sword, an ax,

a wooden bowl with a red candle stump, red plastic flowers, a cigar and a small bottle of rum. In such a manner has Changó, the majestic ruler of fire, thunder and lightning, replaced Jesus. Now I understand the scene back on the porch. The woman in white who rushed out the gate is a practitioner of Santería; the name Yeyé is a repetition of the first two letters in Yemaya, who is Queen of the Waters and mother to Changó.

What had the *santera* whispered to Yeyé and her husband about me? I'm caught up in suspicion and fear—in the power of Santería that ricochets from wall to wall inside my grandmother's empty house.

"A little coffee?" Out comes a thimbleful, and Yeyé sits next to me on the park bench they've set up on the porch.

"Angélica died of stomach cancer. She got all your letters. I read them to her. After I'd finished reading, she used to close her eyes and hold your letter on her lap."

It's more than I can absorb. My throat is closing; my eyes smart. "I'll be back tomorrow. I'll bring coffee and cookies."

"Bring us sugar too."

Sugar? How can there be a house in Cuba without sugar?

The gate creaks the way it did forty years ago. I cup my hand over the hinge to silence the memories. *Walk away! Don't look back!* But also: *Turn around! Look back just once more—for the last time!*

I turn, and the porch is ablaze with unnatural light. The Moorish tiles shine, their geometries cryptic and menacing. Roses are blooming in the flowerbeds, their petals waving like tentacles of sea anemones. Mama Angélica, having risen from the dead, is cooing and applauding from the doorway.

I recoil at the hallucination and turn to flee, but I hear Papa Karman calling. *Come back. Read to me.* He's waving a *Paris Match* with General de Gaulle on the cover.

The past has opened like a sinister flower whose perfume is the allure of madness. I try to struggle out of my vision, pulling my own body up by the roots. Walking among the fallen houses, my legs feel trapped in quicksand. I am going to be annihilated. Changó is witnessing all this—or is he directing?

The hotel elevator spits me out on the fifth floor, and I rush to my room whispering to God. *Señor, Dios mío*, help me remember who I am. Please let me find my sanity somewhere amid my clothes!

⁜ ⁜ ⁜

My first real breakfast in Havana, on a sunlit terrace, is a steaming *café con leche* and the *pan de gloria* I adore, a yolk-yellow sweet bread I haven't tasted for thirty-six years. It's just the tonic I need after Mama Angélica's house, where ghosts run free and Changó is lord of the bedroom.

But ghosts, *my* ghosts, are all over Havana, especially here in the district of El Vedado.

Before we left Cuba for Miami, Houston, Connecticut or Madrid, my friends and I, lively teenagers on the loose, got our fill of life along the sidewalks of La Rampa, just a block away from the hotel. We fed off the *vida loca* that surrounded La Rampa's Radiocentro, a combination movie theater, recording studio, radio station and below-ground cafeteria where we'd heard *bolero* torch singer Olga Guillot, from inside her cloud of ennui, order a sultry chicken croquette. Raquel Revuelta, goddess of the Havana stage—a being made from light and air—once materialized in that place, right in front of us, and ordered *café con leche* with a glass of *agua fría;* we got her to autograph our paper napkins.

Elvira, Zaira, Andrea and I became regular members of La Rampa's sidewalk traffic. We blended in with actors and actresses, crooners, dandies dressed in palm- and flamingo-colored shirts, voluptuous models in tight skirts and low-cut blouses, and neighborhood maids who timed their visits to coincide with the appearances of their favorite soap-opera actors. The sidewalks of La Rampa were tropical Petri dishes where flamboyant forms of life

Raquel Revuelta

Ruston Academy graduation, 1958. From left: Zaira Rodríguez, Elvira Weiss, Andrea Barroso, Olga Karman

swarmed and multiplied. They were a haven for theatrical folk and various wannabes who spoke hackneyed lines in mannered voices and syrupy diction. *Ay, mami, you with all those curves, and me with no brakes.* Here was a display-case for transvestites in high heels; or for slick sugar daddies who wore solid gold on their hairy chests and statuesque women on their arms. La Rampa was the true magnetic north for "nice" girls like us, who weren't allowed to go on dates without chunky chaperones.

For her wedding night, Andrea chose the Havana Hilton Hotel, right across the street from Radiocentro. Elvira, Zaira and I scrutinized the honeymoon suite the day before the wedding. White roses were arrayed in white vases; an ethereal white night-gown was draped across a white satin bedspread. We touched everything, and while Andrea went to get Coca-Colas we gave vent to our jealousy. *What's the point of all that white? So many symbols of virginity just when she's about to lose it.* And we were angry too. How could she abandon our sisterhood just a year out of high school, just when we were ready for real fun?

Next day, when the groom pulled Andrea from the wedding reception, we piled into my Renault and gave chase to the limousine that dangled tin cans from its back fender. We drove onto the La Rampa sidewalk, leaving the car directly below Andrea's window, took off our high heels and waited barefoot for the lights to go off in the honeymoon suite, signaling *the moment of truth.* Would we hear Andrea scream from where we stood on the sidewalk? A small crowd gathered around us and looked up at the hotel window, saying: "Someone might jump!"

And how sweet to remember all this not from Buffalo but a block away from where it happened, standing in the same breeze we had felt while walking on La Rampa and inhaling *la vida loca.*

Another bite of pan de gloria: Father, Roberto and I are at Kasalta Bakery, watching the woman with the tongs lift two glorious loaves from the metal tray. "Separate bags, please," Father asks, so each twin can have one, and he drives us home in the dark gray 1940 Ford with a rod-and-ball floor shift. Every few blocks we see his brown eyes in the rear-view mirror, making sure we don't eat before we get home. As soon as he looks away, we scroll open the bags; keeping our eyes straight ahead, we poke the warm spongy bread and lick the sugar that sticks to our sweaty fingers.

Hey! It's not 1940-something anymore. Go out into the street.

I'll go out, but only after I break this last bit of *pan de gloria* in three—a piece each for Father, Roberto and me.

∗　∗　∗

The ocean is to my left as I walk along the hotel garden path. The stepping-stones are polished coral rocks embedded with ocean fossils: sea fans, sponges, a chambered nautilus, a turban shell. Loveliest of all is a spray of tiny concavities that resembles a miniature fisherman's net suspended in midair. I prolong the walk just as I'd prolonged breakfast. I'm afraid to go out into Havana. I'm safer inside the hotel, sheltered from time and history.

Sheltered from time and history? Who are you kidding? Didn't you see time and history just now, glaring at you from the buffet table?

Pan de gloria has been overshadowed by Eastern European breakfast foods: grated beet and cabbage salad, pickled herring, glasses of liquid yogurt labeled *Yohurt*. Before the Revolution, even right after it, there would have been waffles, pancakes and Aunt Jemima's maple syrup for American tourists. Today, the only audible English comes from two Canadians wearing red maple leaf T-shirts. Once upon a time the United States was a ferry-ride away from Havana. The Revolution has rewritten geography; an abyss now separates my two countries.

An abyss, *un abismo*—that's the word the saleslady at the hotel gift shop uses when she notices me staring at a postcard of a skinny man next to an improbable raft.

"A lot of people buy this rafter one. That ocean where he's headed is an abyss. The sharks know where to wait for us. They know where we cross. The spot is like a trench in the middle of the ocean. That's where we end up. My friend's mother got an arm returned to her. That's what the sharks left of her son."

She asks how long I've been away. When I answer *thirty-six years* she shakes her head and looks down at the floor, just as the guards at the airport did.

"Do you have any family left here?"

"No," I answer. Surprising myself, I add: "You are my family now."

I'm overcome by sadness. In the United States I have my family but I feel like an orphan, bereft of home. In Cuba I have my home but I'm family-poor, and I feel like an orphan here too.

For so long, I've wished I could show my children my home. "This is where I grew up," I would tell them. "These are my streets. These are my people, your people."

The gift-shop lady reaches for my hand. *"Aquí tiene a su familia—Your family is right here."*

Did I corner her into saying that? What did she mean? I look down at her hand resting on mine, at my skin and hers, and I realize she knows me in a way my family in Buffalo will never know me. Language, rituals of affection, city streets whose names we've learned by heart, the marks Cuba has left on us, like tattoos—this is who we are.

❖   ❖   ❖

Before my trip, my friend Emilio, who lives near Buffalo, called two of his friends in Havana, and they promised to take me under their wing. "Tell her to call us from the hotel when she's ready for us to pick her up. Tell her she has to wait for our Lada *outside* the hotel." Now I'm about to meet them.

Halfway into the long hotel drive, a black Lada pulls over but no one steps out. I walk over and, from a short distance, call out: "Are you María Elena?"

A raspy voice answers, "Quick, get in."

Her nervous green eyes dart from the rear-view mirror to the hotel front door. "Call me Mari." She transfers a huge metal lock from the passenger seat onto the rear seat and pulls out at a crawl. "I couldn't pick you up at the door. Cubans aren't allowed near hotels. This is risky. They could charge me with transporting foreigners without a license and take my car away."

Moments later, as we're passing La Rampa, Mari takes a last look in the rear-view mirror and relaxes.

"Antonia and I have already done something more risky. We were at the airport. It was illegal, but we had to try to pick you up. We asked every woman who came out the double doors, 'Are you Olga?' We even asked a man by mistake. He yelled at us: 'No, damn it, I'm not Olga!'"

She laughs with gusto at this bit of absurdity, and her laughter dispels the clouds inside the rickety Lada. There's nothing somber about this woman at all. I sit back, sigh, look out the window and enjoy the breeze on my face.

When we get to her apartment building, she reaches under the dashboard, pulling out a heavy chain and a padlock. "We have to secure the hood from inside when we park, or else they'll steal the battery, the plugs, the fan, the belt." Someone sprang her trunk lock the day before. "Now I have to crawl under the rear of the car to padlock the trunk shut and I will have to go back down again to open it."

On the front steps, a skinny black woman sitting on a wood crate is frying plantain chips over a kerosene burner. *I must be seeing things. A woman cooking on the steps of a building in a fine neighborhood?* She lifts the chips out of the hot oil and slides them into a *cucurucho*—a newspaper cone made from *Granma*, the official newspaper, successor to the paper called *Revolución*. The black lady hands the *Granma* cone to a customer and stretches her neck to receive Mari's kiss on the cheek.

I'm touched by the unassuming harmony of the scene. A week

before my trip, speaking with a Cuban doctor—a good citizen of the Castro regime, who happened to be visiting Buffalo—I asked, "Is there racism in Cuba?" Without missing a beat, the doctor answered: "Blacks are hopeless. They are still swinging from trees. They will always remain marginal to the revolutionary process."

I looked away with shame and sadness. This doctor was a specimen of the "New Man" that the Revolution had promised the world—a man free from the evils of capitalism and imperialism—and he had turned out a troglodyte.

The black woman hands me a *cucurucho*. When I try to pay, she insists "no, no, no," then runs inside and returns with a tiny mound of salt in her cupped hand.

"You see how *Granma* serves us?" Mari says with mock pride. "We use it for *cucuruchos* and toilet paper."

Three deadbolts later, Mari's sister Antonia has unlocked the front door from inside. Stocky, olive-skinned, with dark brown eyes and a mischievous smile, she opens her arms for an *abrazo* and heads straight for the Christmas tree.

"We've set it up year after year, even when they were forbidden. Look at our ornaments, four decades old." It's no exaggeration; with silver-colored birds and bubbling glass candles, this is a Christmas tree from a black-and-white film. On close inspection, I see it isn't a real tree at all; it's a wooden pole covered with foil, and lashed to it for foliage are three-fingered pine branches that twist round and round all the way to the top.

I think of the Christmas tree I've just left in the States. For a moment, Cuba and Buffalo seem to fuse and confuse. Which is real?

Riotously, Mari and Antonia open the gifts I've brought. They hold up the short-sleeved blouses, the makeup kit, the aerosol inhalers for Mari's asthma, magic markers, India ink, crafts magazines for Mari the glassmaker. Mari brings everything to a halt as she disappears into the craft illustrations, turning the pages like a girl with a doll catalog. Almost in passing, she tells me she finds her glass supplies in debris from fallen-down houses. "Antonia and I are experts at picking through rubble. Look at my hands."

She holds them up for me: puffed, blotched, raw not just from debris but also from the chemicals she uses. She can't find gloves in Havana. "Look," she says again, opening her hands and spreading apart the reddened, swollen fingers.

A word of sympathy is on the tip of my tongue, but then my gaze meets her look of triumph, and I realize those hands aren't meant to elicit sympathy. They're meant to show me her spirit. More, they're inviting me to partake of it. Her eyes are searching mine with a simple question: *Are you with me?*

How can I be with you? I don't deserve to be part of your struggle. I left Cuba. I deserted. While I soul-search, her hands are spread open before me, waiting, beckoning me out of my past and into her present. Or is it *our* present? *How can I say no? Maybe it's not a matter of deserving but of having been asked.*

Yes, I'm with you. "Show me where you work. Show me your stained glass." She will, she will, after we talk.

The family photos I've brought whip up a new gust of excitement. My grandsons are in parkas, hats and mittens, peering out of the igloo they've built after a snowstorm; one of them is making a snow-angel. "Will you look at that snow? *Mira,* Olga, that boy looks just like you!"

In our clipped words, in the questions that don't require answers, in our ebullience, I see that while time and history might seem implacable, the human spirit rises above them, impervious as a melody.

Queen Mab's Veil

PALADAR: A HOME RESTAURANT, a type of private enter-prise that the Cuban government began to allow in 1994. Maximum seating permitted: twelve. Neither shrimp nor lobster may be served at a *paladar.*

* * *

A young girl answers the doorbell and leads Mari, Antonia and me upstairs past the bedroom where the *paladar* family is lounging on the bed. They look up, greet us and resume their conversation. Meanwhile, a different youngster recites the *especiales:* fried shrimp, shrimp Creole, pan-fried steak and onions, *congrí* (black beans and rice cooked together), and "enough lobster for one person."

My heart beats faster. *Shrimp and lobster, the forbidden fruits, are on the menu. We haven't been broken.*

Paper napkins on our laps, we begin to tell our stories quickly, interrupting each other as if to hurry our budding friendship. Mari decides that we'll take turns and that I'm first. "No, no, no. You first, or Antonia."

All at once, I'm feeling reticent. I've never told my life to anyone who stayed in Cuba. What right do I have to recount hardships—or worse, to recount moments of happiness in the United States?

"The day I left Havana on the *Guadalupe* my family was standing at La Punta waving handkerchiefs. And then, after we set sail, something awful happened.... Well, I'm never going back to that place."

I describe my first winter in *el Norte*—isolation, sad marriage, overeating. I don't tell them about the razor blades. They approve of my daughter Carla's name: "That could be a Cuban name, *Carla*." I tell them about Connecticut College, and how I got my Spanish back after three years of speaking only English. "Do you think my Spanish is weak?" I ask them parenthetically.

"No. You sound just like us."

Then graduate studies at Harvard—"No! You went to *Harbar? HAR-BAR?* NO!"—my second marriage, my son Nathaniel, whose name they can't pronounce, the move to Buffalo, the second divorce, my children's pain. "I'm good at repeating mistakes," I confess with a shame even more pointed than usual because I'm in Cuba, where once I'd been innocent.

They answer vehemently: "We're good at mistakes too. We *are*. It's not just you!"

I continue. At a difficult period, my children and I are living in such penury that I myself do without dinner and learn to fall asleep hungry; I drink a glass of water and lie on my stomach. One time I actually shoplift snow-boots for Nathaniel. "It was wrong to do that," I tell them, still feeling guilt over my act of thievery thirty years before.

"No! Any mother would have done the same thing!"

Exhausted and a little panicky, I race to a trumped-up ending:

"After my Ph.D. thesis, I get a job and my meteoric rise in life begins." I want to make them laugh, to dispel the cloud I've put over us.

"We didn't know," Antonia whispers, folding and unfolding her paper napkin. "We didn't know life there could be so hard."

They haven't bought my put-on humor. Their sincerity makes me still more ashamed. I reach for my water and choke on the first gulp.

They begin their story slowly, anecdotes first. The Russians have sent a huge shipment of metal colanders to Cuba. *What for? We didn't have any pasta to strain.* So they make lampshades out of the colanders; and when a shipment of toothbrushes arrives they melt them down for earrings.

My companions lower the volume as they move onto sensitive ground. *Confidencial,* they warn me. Even telling this story will place them in danger.

"Years ago we started a clandestine bakery at home; illicit, you know, a business, *un negocio.* Our house became a movie set. In the daytime it was a home; at night we dismantled the home, set up the bakery and got to work. Just before dawn we dismantled the bakery and set up the home again. The flour, the eggs, the sugar, everything was bartered—black market. A friend who worked in a hotel kitchen gave us bags of flour; we drove up to the back door late at night. We traded eggs for housework. Our clients waited for our deliveries with all their lights turned off, and we drove around with the car lights turned off too. The bakery closed down when the gas supply in Havana began to be shut off at night without warning. Our cakes fell; our pies got ruined."

Antonia stops and shakes her head: "*¿Para qué seguir?* Why go on?"

I urge her to continue. She tells of the night Mari almost died during an asthma attack because the aerosol pump at the hospital was broken.

With the anguish and regret I have felt about U.S. policy toward Cuba, I am compelled to ask: "Mari almost died because of the American embargo, right?"

"Don't you believe that, *chica!* Come on, don't talk nonsense! Communism doesn't work, *punto y aparte!*—period and new paragraph!"

They tell of their family, split in half between those who left Cuba and those who stayed to look after failing elders. "By the time Mother and Father died, we were in our forties and it was difficult to leave. Besides," and here Mari looks down, poking at the guava and cream cheese on her plate, "our family in the United States never asked us to come live with them, not even to visit. Our lives can't yet be told fully. Some day ..."

In the silence that follows, I picture the Malecón seawall. It's become our Berlin Wall. On one side, the Cubans who left are severed from their personal histories. They'll never know who they were or who they are. On the other, the Cubans who stayed are pieces of broken families, and they've had decades of grueling hardship. The beautiful Malecón has become our nation's open wound.

Very early in the morning, I've seen flocks of black swans bobbing in that ocean off the seawall; but thinking again, I've realized that swans don't live in oceans. The "swans" are actually inner tubes with men's limbs dangling over the edges.

"They go out every day at dawn to fish," Mari explains, "but they hardly ever catch anything. Those waters have been picked clean."

* * *

"We want to drive you to your house after lunch," Mari says, and when I wince, she offers a postponement: "We can go later, when the sun is lower."

It's too soon to see the house where my brother and I grew up, but *later* comes soon enough. Mari picks up the car keys and we're on Quinta Avenida, awash in deep purple, orange, crimson, soft green, apricot, pink—driving inside a luminous dome where the air itself is spun gold. I remember the Incas' name for the capital of their empire: *Cuzco*, navel. *Havana, you are navel, the center of a luminous universe.*

Lord in Heaven, please help me get through this sunset. Help me see my house again without falling apart.

＊　＊　＊

My house in Miramar was one block from a beach where the ocean was gentle except during hurricanes, when it became raging surf. Waves jumped the breakwater, crossed two streets, rose up over our front steps and came right into our living room. Roberto and I could hydroplane from the sofa to the bookcase where Mother kept her leather-bound *Britannica.* The morning after a hurricane, we hitched rides on passing dinghies and visited neighbors marooned on their porches or, calf-deep in water, pointing at the devastation: downed wires, fallen tree-limbs, big-mouthed baby birds crying inside their broken nests.

Our house had been finished just in time for Roberto and me to come home from the clinic where we'd been born so early and so small that we both fit into the same cradle. Red tile roof, white stucco walls, navy-blue shutters, a deep pink *piscuala* vine that cascaded from the upstairs balcony to the first-floor windows and gave us blossoms for making necklaces and bracelets; that was our house. The entrance was partly hidden behind elephant-ear plants and ground cover that we called *cucarachitas*, "little cockroaches." The orange mimosa stood almost at the curb. In the small back patio were more elephant ears, a papaya tree and a jasmine. Onésima did our laundry back there and hung clothes to dry from ropes that crisscrossed the patio.

Grandfather Terry, my Papa Juan, moved in with us when my brother and I were about sixteen years old. Papa Juan awed us with his eccentricity. He rarely spoke; he hid dinner crackers inside his napkin; he spent his days doing crossword puzzles in English and reading about interplanetary travel. His only author was Jules Verne, his only book *Journey from the Earth to the Moon.* "It's just a matter of time before everything Verne tells us becomes a reality," he told my brother and me. Well into his eighties, Papa Juan got into his gray Packard coupe, took himself to La Concha beach, rowed out far from shore and dove in for a swim.

The little we knew about Papa Juan made no sense to Roberto and me. For years he'd lived in a boarding house we'd never seen, yet his Terry ancestors had been wealthy barons, part of the sugar aristocracy. He worked at something that Mother called "diathermy," which probably paid for the Packard coupe with tortoiseshell dashboard and cashmere-covered seats and his initials 'JAT,' for Juan Andrés Terry, engraved under the door-handles.

A few months after he moved in with us, Papa Juan had a heart attack. Dr. Arístides Menéndez examined his shivering skinny body as we watched his toes turn purple and spread open like the ribs of a fan. *Don't die! We want you with us!* I meant to tell him. "No more going to the beach, Señor Terry!" the doctor ordered. "No more rowing or swimming, not even when the water's warm! You're almost ninety, *por Dios!*"

Coming home from school one day, I found the neighbors standing in front of my house. Mother was crying silently; I noticed her eyes were bluer than ever. Josefina, who lived in the gray stucco house across the street, led me to her porch. "Your dear grandfather died," she told me. "He didn't suffer."

The night of the wake, while Mother and Father were gone, Roberto and I heard the downstairs furniture scraping across the living-room tiles. Next day our maid Juanita, who had found Papa Juan's body hanging from a porch beam, gave us her frightening explanation: "*Míster* Terry is a soul wandering in sorrow because he committed suicide. He'll be like that for a long time."

It was a while before I could pay attention at school. If it rained, I worried that water would seep down into Papa Juan's casket. If it was hot, I worried that his body would decompose before all his senses had quit.

Now, forty years after his death and on my way to the house where he killed himself, I think back to those razor blades lined up on the rim of my bathtub in North Stonington. I came close to doing what Papa Juan had done. I understand him very well. Maybe I'm the one who understands him best.

※　※　※

Back then: my *barrio* was lively with people and car traffic, with voices calling and radios playing. When Roberto and I were little, Pepe Cancio, owner of the corner *bodega*, let the neighbors use one of his storerooms for a kindergarten class. We learned our ABC's from the teacher, who held the big letters high as she wove her way around bags of rice and cans of *chorizo.* We, her pupils, were perched on crates of Malta Hatuey, a syrupy drink that Mother would mix with condensed milk for me so I'd put on a little weight. Two or three doors away, Cervera's busy pharmacy had rocking chairs out in front so people could wait comfortably while he filled their prescriptions. When I got to my teens, those folks in the rocking chairs could watch me push my Scarsdale-bound love letters into the pharmacy's mailbox. Across from Cervera's was Miramar Grocery, scented with *bacalao,* coffee and cigar smoke coming from the cantina, where men rolled dice and drank Hatuey or Cristal beer. *"El gróceri"* was where we watched TV for the first time and marveled that we could see a movie *without going to the movies.* Of course, we could not foresee the starring role that television would soon play in our country's history. By January 1, 1959, almost every urban home had a set that was ready to tune in to Fidel Castro's Revolution-by-TV.

Roberto and I clocked fewer waking hours at home than at

Miramar Yacht Club down the street, where we learned to swim, fish and row. Some Sunday mornings, my boyfriend Raúl Argilagos and I went for a sail. Afterward we sat at the bar sipping daiquiris, munching on fried pork rinds and drifting inside a haze of sea salt, rum, lime, sugar, and teenage passion before we parted to go home for lunch.

Long before those teenage years, I was part of that flock of little girls whose mothers or nursemaids, *tatas,* toweled us dry after swimming lessons, then sprinkled us with violet-scented water and talcum powder, dressed us quickly so that we wouldn't catch cold, braided our hair and snapped our barrettes closed. Sunlight streaming through the high locker-room windows, the scent of violet water, docile girls stepping into their clothes as dreamily as cranes—this scene from "yesterday's Cuba" might have been happening in the 19th century.

If I'd been one of those *tatas,* would I have been glad the Revolution had come, or would I be longing for "yesterday's Cuba"? All of us were figures in a tapestry that history had begun to weave the day Columbus landed. When the Revolution came, I hoped we could reweave that tapestry and create a better design. So many times I've asked myself: If I'd stayed in Cuba, could I have made a difference? Now, looking around Havana, I wonder: How could I have made a difference in *that?*

Not all *barrio* memories are sweet. Patricio and Tony de la Guardia, the other set of neighborhood twins, a year older than we and nicknamed *las urracas,* "the magpies," because they looked like Heckel and Jeckel, joined Fidel's government: Colonel Tony de la Guardia and General Patricio de la Guardia. After they had done the regime's bidding for thirty years, Fidel charged Tony with drug trafficking and sent him to the firing squad, while Patricio got a thirty-year prison term.

But it's the less blatant suffering of my old *barrio* that brings me the greater sorrow. How naïve we all were to take its permanence and our presence there for granted, even if it's hard to see how we could have done otherwise. Our neighborhood families—Astorgas, Díaz Sera, Mesa, Cancio, Salup, Martínez-Ybor, Castroverde—had never moved into or out of the *barrio;* we'd all been there, or so it seemed, forever. If not precisely logical, it was sensible to believe that Señor Mesa would forever walk around in his underwear looking out his window when he needed to holler at the parrots and macaws in his aviary—*"¡Cállense, carajo!* Shut Up, damn it!"*—himself becoming a macaw; that Josefina Díaz Sera would spy on teenagers into eternity; that Clarita and Julián Salup, who owned the cream-colored Packard, would enjoy their breakfast *café con leche* on the porch until they switched venues and took breakfast in Heaven. All of us were fixed stars in the same firmament. So were the vendors whose calls made us run out into the street and flag them down:

"¡PECAO FLECO—Fresh Fish!" That's the call of "Manuel the Chinaman," who carries a metal picnic basket with red snapper and yellowtail between layers of shaved ice. He'll scale and gut fish on the curb, surrounded by a pack of agitated cats including our Cusita.

¡MANGO, MANGUEEÉ! That's the fruit man seated high up on a mule-cart decorated with palm leaves. He's got mangoes, *mameyes, anones* displayed on shiny banana leaves. His mule's coat reflects the sun like a jet-black mirror. The animal smells sweet; I know because I press my nose to her neck and inhale. Her hooves are painted with clear enamel. I tap her leg and she picks it up for me to inspect.

"¡AFILADOOOOOR. AFILO CUCHILLO, TIJERA! I am the sharpener! I sharpen knives and scissors!" This intrepid craftsman blows some *do re mi fa sols* on his tiny harmonica to entice us outside with our cutlery so that he can sharpen it on his huge rotating stone-on-wheels—a tricycle-like contraption that he pushes along the *barrio* streets. The sharpener scares me.

"GOOD AFTERNOON," in English, says "Josephine the Jamaican," who's at our front door in white nurse's uniform and

white hairnet. She's hoping Mother will come out and chat with her in English. Josephine lifts her picnic basket flap and shows off fruit tarts—guava, mango, lemon, pineapple—all the while standing at attention with metal tongs up in the air, waiting for us to choose.

"BONJOUR. BONJOOUUUURR." That's François the Frenchman, who wears a Panama hat, sells fresh produce and eggs, and chats Mother up in French while Juanita, hidden behind the curtains, whispers to me: *"Mira, el francés de los huevos*—Look! The Frenchman with eggs"—which in Cuban slang also means "the Frenchman with balls"—and we laugh uproariously.

That laughter comes back to haunt me when Tío Miguel buys twenty Leghorn hens and I become his door-to-door egg-rep as well as the neighborhood maids' laughingstock. When I ring their doorbells carrying their egg-orders in brown paper bags, they cry out, *"¿Quién es?* Who is it?" And I have no choice but to answer, *"Olguita, la niña de los huevos*—Olguita, the girl with balls."

And then, in 1959, the diaspora begins. Ready or not, all those neighbors who have never known uprooting begin to up-root. We turn each other's quintessential gestures into memories so that we'll never lose each other completely. Señor Mesa is forever screaming; Josefina is spying; Clarita and Julián are delicately dunking; and Raúl Argilagos, my *novio,* is reading the direction of the wind on a bit of red yarn he's tied to the mast of his sailboat, *Rascacio*—squinting into eternity with zinc oxide dabbed on his nose and the tips of his ears.

*   *   *

We're still a few blocks away from my house but Mari is slowing down, white-knuckled at the wheel, staring straight ahead. I see them now: armed men in black uniform posted on every corner. With machine-gunned syllables, Mari whispers: "Fidel's special guard—the only people in Cuba who eat fillet of beef. He must be right near here." The sinister men in black stare deeply into the car as we drive by; they violate whatever they see and fill us with dread. Mari begins to wheeze but doesn't pull over until the men in black have disappeared from the rear-view mirror. It's an asthma attack; she takes out the inhaler, uses it, stops, picks it up again, works with it. *Can she breathe yet? So this is life in Havana.* My saliva turns thick.

⁎ ⁎ ⁎

A sharp left, a right, and I spot her: my house. Can this be my street? It's deserted, silent. I feel as if I'm swimming under water with plugs in my ears. *Never mind. Here she is. Mi casa. Mi amiga. They've painted you cornflower blue, just like Onésima's bluing cubes. How pretty you look in blue.*

Conchita Food Products, a large sign in front proclaims. *Conchita* used to mean and apparently still means a compote of guava marmalade, grated coconut and grapefruit shells in heavy syrup. *Mi casa, the Revolution has sweetened you.* I want to run inside; but when we walk up to the door, the man in charge meets us with an inhospitable silence followed by a blunt command: "*Diga.* You may speak."

"I lived here long ago. May I come in?"

Grim silence; he's doing his best to stare me down, but over his shoulder I see my house begin to sway just as a curvy Gaudí house appears to sway; it's signaling *welcome home.* If it had arms, they would be open wide.

"Wait here," the man orders. He returns and ushers us in. "I'm giving you five minutes. You can't go upstairs."

I want to touch, but don't dare, the wrought-iron porch door to which Roberto and I clung for support when we were learning to walk. I want to see the toilet we used to plug with small juice glasses so that the plumber would come with his bag of interesting tools. I walk on the tiles where we practiced rock 'n' roll steps. I try to peek into what was once the kitchen so that I can see the counter where my boyfriend Benito nibbled on my earlobe, knowing we were safe as long as Mother was in the living room listening to Fidel. I want the dining-room table back in place, with Alvarito, Fiti-Coco and Vivian playing Monopoly and dunking Galleticas de María into hot cocoa because it's winter.

"Please step outside now." Mari and I cross the street for one last look. I'm noticing that I don't feel anger or resentment, but rather joy and an irrational certainty; the blue house has recognized me. We're standing right in front of Josefina's gray stucco house. Her high garden wall is gone and so is the garden, with Don Pepe's lime trees. In its place a *paladar* has sprung up: *Paladar la Mulata*, The Mulatto Lady's Restaurant. The Mulatto Lady herself is at the bar wiping the counter, trying not to be obvious; but then she says rather obviously, "We make the best black beans and rice in Miramar," and hands me a business card with a palm tree arched over the *paladar's* name and address.

I look up and down my empty street, seeing the lime trees, the de la Guardia magpies, the firing squads taking aim, the disappeared: Raúl, Ignacito, Vivian, Waldito, Fiti-Coco, all of them gone—gone where? The only ones left are the *paladar* woman and the dour Conchita man. The absurdity of our history smacks me. How senseless, what's happened to Cuba! What good has all this done? I look back at my house one last time.

Papa Juan, can you see me? I'm back. I'm on my own journey from the Earth to the Moon.

※　※　※

Long after dark I return to my hotel room hungering for solitude and a counterbalance to the weight pressing on my heart. The joy I felt in Miramar has left me, and a ponderous gloom is in its place. My house and Mama Angélica's are peopled by our own ghosts. I'm afraid I might be falling apart. Mama and Papa

Karman standing on their porch, risen from the dead—my house swaying and yearning to embrace me—isn't that proof enough? Only Mari and Antonia seem solid. They are my horizon in Havana.

* * *

Secure inside my bedroom, I've stored more than enough for dinner: Galleticas de María, guava paste, a breakfast *pan de gloria* that I've wrapped in a napkin just as Papa Juan used to wrap his dinner crackers—all of it safe from marauding *cucarachas*.

The ocean's night breeze puffs up the curtains and rummages in my things as if looking for something. Five flights down, a trio playing on the hotel terrace draws me to the window, where I gaze over the water, the seawall, the Malecón Boulevard. Where once lines of cars and crowds of people were going places, what a stillness now presides! All I see are a few bicycles and the dim headlights of a vintage car approaching at a crawl. *Havana, my city of lights, you've gone dim.*

The trio on the terrace is singing Olga Guillot's *"Miénteme"*—"Lie to Me." The first line, "I'm learning to live off your lies," is a zinger; and then there's the gutsy ending we so enjoyed as teenagers: "Lie to me more! Your wickedness makes me happy."

Mentiras, lies: that's me deluding myself, thinking I can join the present to the past the way you graft a shoot to a full-grown plant. It's not going to take. No one in Havana carries my last name; no one knows me except Father's ninety-year-old cousin Eduardito, and even he will not smell a family member in me. After all, it's been four decades.

A Latin phrase drifts into my memory, a paper plane made from words: *Non omnis moriar.* "I will not die completely"—Horace, Latin 101. His poems, Horace said, would be more enduring than bronze, *aere perennius.* In some small way, they would keep him living. Will this small witness I bear keep some of our past from dying completely?

What is all the gloom and doom? For God's sake, chica, *carpe diem, seize the moment, forget history, forget time, feed on Havana as the parrotfish feeds on coral. Forget the fossils and take heart.* Mañana será otro día—*tomorrow is another day.*

Mañana is the problem. Every *mañana* takes its bite.

*   *   *

And then Queen Mab from her carriage made of a single pearl picked up a blue veil, almost impalpable, as if composed of sighs or of dreamy blond angels' gazes. And that veil was the veil of dreams, of the sweet dreams that make life seem rose-colored. And with it she wrapped up the four skinny, bearded, impertinent men, a sculptor, a painter, a musician, and a poet, who stopped being sad because hope had entered their hearts, and the cheerful sun entered their heads along with that little devil vanity, *which consoles poor artists in the depths of their disappointment.*

—from "Queen Mab's Veil," a story by Rubén Darío (my translation)

*   *   *

Mañana is here. Mari's Lada is waiting discreetly half a block from the hotel.

"I thought today we could go to *La Habana Vieja.*" Her delicacy, asking permission to give me a full day in the Old City, moves me. My affection for her is growing by the minute. It's a good thing; all we have are minutes.

All the way to the Malecón we go, and then we veer inwards. We plunge into Old Havana along the streets Father and I traveled when I worked at Casa Karman. *You're with me, Papi. We're here together.* Mari is naming what we see: *balustradas, marquetería, fosos, baluartes, soportales*—Old Havana's balustrades, marquetry, moats, bulwarks, columned galleries. We sip *La Habana Vieja's* nectar, flower by flower, like two honeybees. The sound of the open vowels in *mamparas, aldabas, persianas*—the music for col-ored-glass panes—is almost too intoxicating. Leaves and flowers etched on the colored glass flash their ruby-red, indigo, emerald-green and mustard-yellow doubles onto walls and floors; their shadows shift with the hours, marking time. These are hourglasses made from sunlight.

Mari points toward La Punta and I look away, down at the ground, and follow her into El Castillo de La Fuerza, the 16th-century fortress that the Spaniards built to protect Havana from pirates. From its towers, the watch could see the galleon fleet sailing toward Havana for repairs and provisions before the voy-age back to Spain. In the ships' holds: Aztec and Inca gold and silver, "Indians" to take back to the king and queen, large brown leaves called *tabaco.* Mari positions me so that I can "see" the ships, and I do, calling to mind our history, feeling it alive inside the damp walls of the narrow circular staircase we climb to the lookout. "The stone is twenty feet thick." We wind our way sky-ward as if inside a giant chambered nautilus, and all of a sudden we're high up on a terrace, wrapped in ocean breeze, looking down on the oldest section of the city, the narrow streets and the pastel blue balconies hanging from lemon-yellow façades. Purple bou-gainvillea crowds filigreed gates; stone curls and drapes over porticoes with a silken ease.

I've lived to see all this again. If only I could show it to Carla and Nathaniel!

Another part of Havana comes into view—a hell into which I stumble only a block away: rubble, walls blackened with soot, rotting garbage heaped against curbs, stagnant water in deep pot-holes. Havana is crumbling onto its sidewalks.

"Is there still time left to save the city?" I ask Mari as we're picking our way amid litter and fetid water.

"We've run out of time," she answers without looking at me. "It's too late."

Before I've had time to let *too late* sink in, we're inside another magnificent courtyard. But I've had enough of architecture. *I just want my darkened hotel room,* I'm telling myself as a shirtless man rushes up to us—no escaping him—and stands inches from my face demanding to know who I am, why I'm carrying a notebook. Am I a government official? I explain I'm visiting from the United States and writing down everything so that I don't forget.

He grabs me by the wrist. "Well then, follow me," and he climbs over the rubble on the stairs, up to the second floor where he points at walls and ceilings. "Write down everything you see. Look at the holes in the walls. Look at the roof. See? See the sky? Next rainstorm, this roof is going to collapse. Then they'll haul us away to the compound where they pen the homeless like animals. Write that in your notebook. Tell them all this when you go back."

He looks over my shoulder, making sure I write all of it.

By the time we walk outside, I'm shaking. The sun and heat suffocate me; the dusty sidewalk rises toward my face.

Mari's voice becomes barely audible. What I hear now is the voice of my own memory reciting history lessons, geography lists, names of Cuban rivers that fifth-grade teacher Señora Rosario arranged for us in rumba tempo: *CabreraYariguá ChaparraMayarí SaguadeTánamo MoaToa DuabaMiel.* Then come the names of the little bones of the hand, *falange falangina falangeta,* and the entire taxonomy of mammals we learned in eleventh grade: *bimanos, monos, carnívoros, insectívors, digitígrados, plantígrados, roedores, xenartros, artiodáctilos, perisódactilos, proboscidios, sirenios, cetáceos, marsupiales, y monotremas.*

I'm under assault by mental debris: a Spanish-language *danse macabre* with music and words made up from decades of flotsam.

Without English, who am I after all these years? What am I in Spanish but a tentative girl raising her hand in class? Who am I in Spanish but a fifty-six-year-old Cuban woman whom no one in Cuba recognizes. I'm nobody. Who are you?

A big open space—oh, thank God—air! We're in a vast art studio, a warehouse with printmakers and lithographers working at tables that face the Cathedral Plaza.

Young apprentices stand silently at attention next to their *maestros,* oozing *respeto.* One of them, Paneka, kisses Mari and shows us a set of five-foot-tall cards he's engraved for the Tarot Society. At the next full moon, he himself will place them inside a tent with a hole in the top so that they fill up with moon power. "Have to follow Tarot Society rules," he explains with a wry, iconoclastic, 100-percent Cuban smile that restores some of the life I lost on the street. A black man at the next table, "Chocolate," is working on a collage made of crushed soda-pop cans he's found on the street, while another man they call "Chucho" is carrying a drawing to the ancient-lithography press as ceremoniously as if it were a sacred scroll.

I imagine Queen Mab's veil suspended over these men, making them immune to Havana's hardships. If I were to ask, "Would you want to be somewhere else?" they might reply, "What for?" Under Queen Mab's veil, even their Havana seems rose-colored.

Where Have They Gone?

WHAT A STORM! THE WIND blows the heavy drapes parallel to the floor; lightning zigzags inside my room. In this wonderful upheaval, who can sleep? I'll open *Los rituales del inocente*—The Innocent's Rites—a book that poet Lina de Feria gave me earlier. It'll be like opening the Bible at random, hoping the passage I find is destined for me.

No time to sleep now;
let us move on toward the wellsprings
now that the end of the century
is really dying.

No time to sleep when lightning is crashing, and the 20th century is surely dying—but where are Cuba's wellsprings?

Electric charges in the shapes of root-systems are exploding across the sky, dangling in the black air. The charges blow out my old synapses, and rather than dwell on my old *barrio* I think about the claims of the present: Mari and Antonia, or my broken Havana five floors below. Are they the wellsprings that will slake my thirty-six-year-old thirst?

Lina, you're casting for hope, while I see hopelessness every-where. On the Malecón, street-walking *jineteras* in spandex mini-skirts strut after dark waiting for a john who's gross and impolite and speaks in a foreign tongue. But the frog might be a prince, the way to a new life abroad, or at least a pile of *dólares,* food for the children and husband waiting at home, for a new spandex so that the huntress can go out again to look for prey.

Remembering the past is no match for what these souls must endure. It is no match for the man I saw lying on his back under a parked car, siphoning gasoline into a bottle so that he could sell it for a few pesos; or for the young woman, slumped on a stair-case landing, who said, "I'm anemic, but the doctor at the *policlínica* told me there wasn't any B12 left in all Havana." It is no match for the man pedaling slowly next to me and whispering what I thought were compliments that made no sense. And then I understood what he was whispering. *Kitchen cleanser? Chicken bouillon cubes? Powdered milk*? He was trying to sell me whatever he'd stolen, bartered or borrowed. Painful memories pale next to the father sitting on his front stoop and talking to the son who drowned in the Florida Straits: "Watch that wave, Nando. Look behind you. *Cuidado con esa ola."* Forget the past, and read again the prisoner's letter that someone gave you to keep:

"I need an inhaler and a blanket because my asthma gets bad at night in the cold cell and we have no covers. I'm hungry. All they give us is cabbage soup and a little rice."

My disembodied past is nothing compared to the *ancianos* on the street—old people with their useless bodies still attached to them.

My father's cousin Eduardito might be one of these.

* * *

What will Eduardito look like? What will I look like to him? The last time he saw me I was twenty. I'm close to sixty now. I won't tell him Papi's dying. I've brought him *dólares, dólares*. That's what he asked for when I called him from Buffalo. But I want to bring him food. Mari and I stop for groceries at one of the stores Havana calls "La Shopping" because the windows used to say **SHOPPING** when only foreigners with dollars could go inside. Now dollars are legal, and anyone with dollars can shop at "La Shoppings." That means foreigners or Cubans with family members in exile who send them dollars. The irony escapes no one: the masses of true believers don't have currency to shop, while counterrevolutionaries fill their baskets.

First, the basics: bread, a chicken, rice, oil, canned vegetables, real coffee instead of peso-store coffee cut with ground chickpeas. Then the extras: chocolate kisses, Galleticas de María cookies, a slab of traditional Christmas nougat, a wedge of brie. Mari is standing at a distance, her eyes fixed on me and my cart. On the way to the car, she whispers, "Be prepared for a shock, Olga. Old people here are desperate."

She has to be wrong. Old people might be desperate, but not my *old people.*

* * *

I spot him, Eduardito, waving something from the third-floor balcony and pointing at a space for us to park even though there are no other cars at the curb. He comes into focus: gaunt, wearing a torn black jacket despite the oppressive heat, with a wool scarf wrapped around his neck. He's waving a long rag, as if he were a castaway. *Rescue me.*

We enter a pitch-dark entrance hallway and mount a pitch-dark stairwell. Light sockets are empty; walls are lined with greasy soot that my fingers pick up when I reach out for balance as we climb toward the sound of his voice. Then we nearly bump into his stubble and blackened teeth. Tatters dangle from his sleeves. Next to him, neatly dressed, is an unsmiling woman in her late fifties. The lady introduces herself: she is *Fe*, Faith. Standing on tiptoe behind her is a beautiful, sullen teenager in black spandex. *A jinetera? Does Father's cousin have a jinetera living in his apartment?*

"*Pasen.*" Eduardito shows us into a big room with two massive carved mahogany tables, one piled high with medical books of a uniform brown—Eduardito was once a physician—and the other table, where he leads us, littered with papers, soiled plates and fruit flies scurrying over a half-eaten bun. Center stage is the rusted refrigerator that he opens, *voilà,* to show its empty insides. We unload the groceries to the tones of Eduardito's recitation; he announces each package, can and jar-label as ceremoniously as if he were welcoming dignitaries.

And then, oblivious to the big flies crawling up and down his sleeves, he begins to speak. "These are the very clothes I was wearing when my blessed mother Conchita died three years ago." My eyes scan the dark jacket shiny with grease, mended sloppily with bright red and yellow threads. As if addressing a multitude, he raises his arms to speak: "Over these very clothes, I put on my old doctor's robe and ministered to her. Her doctors greeted me as a colleague."

Poor, poor ragman, my family ragman, what an apparition you must have been when you walked into that hospital ward. Did they laugh behind your back? Did they gown you to mock you?

He shifts to an unexpected topic: my inheritance.

"Your grandmother Angélica left 40,000 *pesos.* I can account for all of it. The people who took care of Angélica spent all but the last 700. Those I owe you. The cadaver was still warm when Yeyé and her husband came banging on the door demanding the silver that Angélica had given me for safekeeping. There's nothing left of it, *absolutamente nada.* And one more thing: your great-uncle Carlos, Tía Maria's husband... HAH! Carlos got himself married *post mortem.* He'd hired a housekeeper, and his body was still warm when the lawyer got going. *Voilá:* the lawyer 'proved' that the housekeeper and Carlos had been married for years. So, nothing there either. Follow me. I'll take you on a tour of my modest apartment. Let us begin our tour."

With that he rises and Fe disappears, perhaps feeling self-conscious after those stories about Yeyé and Tío Carlos. Maybe she too is waiting for her prey to finish dying. I feel Mari grab my arm. *Why is she steadying me?* First, the kitchen: there's a coconut on a cracked counter, nothing more. Then the spandex-girl's room; it's freshly painted, with a plaid bedspread and a stereo. Eduardito opens the door to his bedroom. Mari's grip tightens as we step into the dim cell. This is not a room where my family member sleeps every night; it is a dingy hole with a bare mattress, blackened by grime, scrunched up against a wall. Clothes are strewn about and flies are crawling all over them, buzzing with excitement about something; perhaps excrement. Mari squeezes my arm harder, distracts me.

Back at the table, Eduardito offers us a coffee and recounts his mother's last years. He speaks in a bizarre 17th-century Spanish. "Calm thyself. Seat thyself," he tells me when I try to give him a hug of condolence for his mother's death. "You can find my mother and the rest of us in the Cementerio de Colón. We're all behind the city firemen's monument." He rises and beckons us to the wall where he has nailed discolored pictures of saints. One of these figures points at his chest wounds, another wields a sword; a woman saint has her eyes turned to Heaven and her foot on a snake. Eduardito narrates the saints' feats and enumerates their powers with a simple faith worthy of Don Quijote.

Eduardito is a specter. Mother is dead, Father is dying and Eduardito is next. Then comes me. The cemetery plot is ready. I think I need some air.

From his terrace, Eduardito waves the same rag goodbye. After we turn the corner, Mari parks the Lada in the shade and turns off the motor. We sit in silence; her company is a consolation. I search for a way to rescue Eduardito, but every idea is futile. And then something not unlike anesthesia slows my dead-end thoughts, taking the edge off what I've just seen. Maybe that's the way you survive in Havana. You wait for the numbness to set in, and then you keep going.

❖ ❖ ❖

As if she'd known what the visit would be like, Antonia has prepared a sensational lunch. The table is set with a faded blue tablecloth and a cluster of pastel blue *embeleso* flowers in a water glass. She brings out *picadillo,* ground beef and pork mixed with olives, raisins and spices; rice; cassava in oil, lime juice and garlic; a bowl of avocado and pineapple chunks in oil and vinegar. To get all this she must have gone from neighbor to neighbor bartering and cashing in old favors. Mari and I oooh and aaahh, praising her. We take our places, and I follow their lead when they bow their heads. Their hands reach for mine. I listen for a prayer of thanksgiving, but Mari asks for something else. "*Señor,* please take care of Olga's Eduardito. You see how he lives, and we can't help him. Please come to his aid." We're three sisters at the family table praying and squeezing hands, *Amén.*

❖ ❖ ❖

The sun is still quite high, but Mari and I can't wait to get to the Cementerio de Colón. Just as Eduardito said, our family tombs, all above ground, are right behind the firemen's monument: Tío Raúl, who played piano rags and died young; great-uncle Carlos and Tía María side by side; Eduardito's mother Conchita, Mama Angélica and Papa Karman all in a row. A wave of joy catches me by surprise when I run my fingers over their names and address them in silence: *Tío Raúl, Tío Carlos, Tía María, Tía Conchita, Mama, Papa Karman, I'm up here. I came back from the United States to see you.*

The sun is a blowtorch but I don't want to leave. There's no place where Mari and I can sit and talk except right on top of one of our tombs. I choose Mama Angélica's, climb up and pat the marble to invite Mari. *Please come here. This is the only place I can offer you in Havana.* We sit cross-legged as if the tomb were Mama Angélica's porch and Mama herself were just a few rooms away napping after lunch, beneath the portrait of Jesus pointing to his sacred heart. Mari tells me what she hadn't at the *paladar.*

"My life has been a series of goodbyes. You don't know what it's like. One by one, best friends and relatives ring the doorbell and tell us they're leaving. All I have to do now is look into their eyes and I know. I've become expert at spotting the *I'm leaving* look."

Then I tell her what I too had held back: the day I left Cuba, the ocean had beckoned me to jump off the deck of the *Guadalupe.* "I couldn't bear seeing La Punta again. I'm afraid of that ocean. It could kill me."

I recite Mari a poem I'd written some 17 years earlier, in 1980:

> *Twenty years later*
> *you dream you go back*
> *looking for the family graves.*
> *You sort through scattered bones*
> *light as the bones of birds now,*
> *filled with air.*
> *You dream you lay a heavy white cloth*
> *on a long table*
> *set among the graves.*
> *You ring the silver bell*
> *for Angélica and Roberto,*
> *for Miguel and Consuelo,*
> *for Raúl.*
> *You ring for your dead*
> *and wait.*

Mari says: "We had no idea—no idea that the ones who left miss us as much as we miss them."

The sun has turned Mari's arms bright pink. I press my thumb into her skin; the spot turns white and then bright pink again. *This proves she's not a ghost but flesh-and-blood. I've rung the silver bell for the dead and for the living.*

＊　＊　＊

A gray-haired, shabbily dressed, much-too-thin figure appears at the end of a long corridor, motionless. The figure stares right at me, and when she begins to approach the light becomes a fine haze. This apparition takes my breath away.

"That's Raquel Revuelta," my companion whispers.

Raquel Revuelta! How lackluster anything I say will seem to those who've seen her on stage.

A long, long time ago: when we were teenage girls, Raquel Revuelta was Cuba's *prima donna,* cultural icon, archetype, feral feminine whose gestures we tried to imitate. Her eyes were ablaze when she was Desdemona, Helen of Troy, Antigone; her dark eyebrows were all vehemence. When in a moment of passion she raised the right brow—it was always the right one—I almost wanted to dive for cover under my seat.

The long corridor has become a stage because she's there. We stand face to face, her piercing gaze pinning me down as if I were a butterfly on the page of her collector's album.

"May I help you with anything at all?" the apparition says.

That voice, that timbre! How dare I deploy my own paltry sounds? But look! Look at her. Look at her ragged clothes. How downtrodden she looks, how defeated.

As if she'd heard me, she raises her head ever so slowly, arches the right brow, and the pride I once adored becomes gesture, serving notice that Cuba's appalling history has left Raquel Revuelta intact.

She knows I'm under her spell, and prolongs the silence. How to answer her? I want to confess everything I've lived since *a long, long time ago:* the losses, the mistakes, the bewilderment. I want to ask her I don't know what; anything to keep her a little longer.

"What is your name?" I say.

"Raquel," she answers with a hint of a wry smile. She's on to me.

Before I know what I'm doing, my hand is rising toward her face; my thumb is tracing the outline of her right brow as lovingly as if she'd been sister or mother. "There's only one person in the world with eyebrows like these. I wanted to be you when I was young."

Our eyes well up. She embraces me but at once regains her composure to deliver her parting line: "Come, come. Let's not become sentimental." And then she disappears.

                    ✵   ✵   ✵

I have been the dreamer of Cuban shadows, but I too have been a shadow. Standing in that Vedado corridor, a witness to Raquel Revuelta's reincarnation, I have become flesh; I have become blood.

                    ✵   ✵   ✵

Two young men walking along the Prado Boulevard are eating something out of a paper cone. It looks and smells good.

"What's that you're eating?"

"Have a taste," they insist.

This is something new: fried potato slices covered with mustard. "*Yumi, yumi.*" We chew and slurp, take turns at a single paper napkin, do a little dance when a dollop of mustard lands on my blouse.

I overhear Mari: "Come on, Antonia, you know what those *papas fritas* cost those boys. They're luxury items, *chica!* She shouldn't have accepted them. Those two are hungry, like the rest of us. Period, new paragraph!"

We walk away from the Prado in cold silence. On to the next *must see,* a church with "amazing catacombs." The sunny court-yard holds a small crowd; people are stuffing things into paper bags and milling around a young woman who's giving orders. "I'm Milagros." I brace myself; her name is "Miracles." What next?

"These are my volunteers," Milagros says. "They're filling care packages with whatever food and medicine they've been able to beg, steal or barter for the *barrio* children and old people. Every-one is needy, but children and old people are the worst off."

"What can I bring you when I come back next year?"

Milagros doesn't even have to think. "Write this down in your notebook."

> *Something to kill head-lice*
> *Anti-parasite medicine (to cure amoebas and giardia)*
> *Pediatric doses of immunoferon*
> *Anti-diarrhea medication*
> *Medication for vascular accidents: Nipodipine,*
>   *captopril, peroxide*
> *Asthma inhalers (salbutamol)*
> *Antihistamines*
> *Pediatric vitamins*
> *B1, B6, B12*
> *Calcium*
> *Remedies to cure mange (pediatric doses)*

"Mange?" I say incredulously.

"Yes," she answers without flinching. "Children in Havana have mange and lice and parasites and diarrhea, and no medicine."

* * *

I make up an excuse and hurry back to my hotel room. Vir-ginia, the chambermaid, is just walking out my door. *"Buenos días, Mami."* My first day in Havana, she called me "Milady," "Olga" the next. Yesterday I gave her a doll for her daughter Viviana. It took some doing to get her to accept it, and when she did she called me *Mami.*

I undress, pitch my clothes into the bag I'm using as a hamper and notice that all my laundry is gone, everything I've worn since leaving Buffalo. Virginia? Everything is in place inside the closet and drawers. Why would she steal my dirty clothes? The bathroom door is shut. *Someone's in there.*

Hanging from the shower-curtain rod—washed, dried and pressed—are all my missing clothes.

⁎   ⁎   ⁎

Havana has worn me out. Mange, horror, peace of mind, joy, hallucinations, reincarnations, *Lie to me more,* mustard caking under my fingernails, a stranger demanding that I "write everything down," Changó's altar, the *paladar mulata,* the black swans off the Malecón, Eduardito's mattress. This morning I overheard a man say: "After I saw an arm and then a leg float by, I turned my raft around and headed back to Havana." And on 25th Street a woman was chatting with her friend. "My husband said, 'Buy fish and wash it before I get home.' 'What fish?' I told him. 'There are no fish left in Cuba. And how am I going to wash it anyway? There's no water either.' "

I don't want any more experiences. On my last afternoon in Havana, any excuse to flee from Mari's house will do. *"Ay, Dios mío,* five o'clock. I've got to pack for tomorrow." But for the heat, I would've broken into a jog after she closed the door.

Midway down the block, the sound of someone whistling a familiar melody brings me up short. When I turn to look for the whistler, no one notices me. No one even seems to see me.

They can't see me because I look like them. I'm swimming with my school of fish.

I hear the soles of my slipper-sandal *chancletas* hitting the sidewalk *clac, clac, clac,* and I hear the other women's *chancletas, clac clac clac;* all of us sway as we go, all of us propelled by the same music, caught up in one languid, rich rhythm. I let my belly stick out, let my *chancletas* make their noise. The *Vogue* photographs I've carried inside my head—wire-thin women who look like soldiers—slide down to the pavement. *We are the paradigm now. Our walk is the walk, our bodies the bodies, our ambling stride just right.* My little potbelly and my *clac clac clac chancletas* lead me on to the traffic light, where I turn and see myself, not quite a woman yet, heading right toward me, coming to find me. She disappears into me, and finally I am at rest, I am made one, as if those forty years away from home have been just a short walk around the block and the traffic light has never changed.

A sassy old song goes off in my head and leads me along the sidewalks of La Rampa:

"Antonio's woman walks like *this,* she walks like *this,* walks like *this....*"

La mujer de Antonio camina así ... ca mi na sí, ca mi na sí, ca mi na sí.

* * *

This same day in Santa Barbara, after lunch, an attendant who's gone into Father's room to check on him returns to the nurses' station. "Mr. Karman must have died in his sleep."

* * *

My last night in Havana. A little scared to be in a taxi by myself, a little self-conscious, I ask the driver: "Take the Malecón, then go up the Prado to the Capitol." Inside the Lada, the ocean air is heavy.

Who remembers how Havana glowed at night long ago; the crowds that filled theaters, nightclubs, bars; entire families strolling arm in arm and taking the breeze? Who remembers the light-garlands from topmast to deck on the docked cruise ships and the birthday parties at El Pacífico in Chinatown? A cage-elevator carried us past a hazy second floor where we could see Chinese men in undershirts playing mahjongg, and then on the third floor our waiters in slippers and pajamas served us platters of sizzling hot fried wontons. "Fried little butterflies," *maripositas fritas*, we called them; and the waiter called them *malipositaflita*.

＊　＊　＊

"Papi, Papi, take us to the Prado; take us to see the Jantzen diver," my brother and I begged in twin duet, and Papi drove all the way from Miramar to the neon bathing-suit billboard perched high above Prado and Neptuno. There she was, the neon diver, so real in her red bathing suit and bathing cap, climbing up the neon ladder rung by rung, taking one, two, three steps along the blue neon diving board, raising her arms, diving into the night, disappearing into a neon pool and then resurfacing to begin her climb back up the neon ladder.

We could count on the Jantzen diver. She stood for beautiful ideals—predictability, permanence, forever—that we had not yet lost.

＊　＊　＊

Where are all the lights? Into my mind comes the Latin phrase that ancient people spoke when they saw the ruins of a city: *Ubi sunt?*

The chauffeur drives at a crawl along the darkened Prado, snickering at the *jinetera* streetwalker who looks into the taxi when we stop at an intersection. It's the darkness itself he's addressing when he makes the old Cuban remark: "It's just like a wolf's mouth."

The Embarcation

*I*T'S OVER. I'M PACKED *and ready.*
  One last look out the hotel-room window: it's a cold, gray morning. A *norte* storm has come in overnight, and waves are exploding against the Malecón.

The phone rings. It's Mari.

"We can't let you go to the airport in a taxi. Antonia and I are driving you. We'll just drop you off and keep on going."

Why? Only yesterday we said goodbye and mapped out our future, vowing to write each other. Someday soon, *soon,* they will visit me in Buffalo. *We'll sit in your garden and talk and talk.* I don't want another *adiós*—but now I've got one.

When we get to the corner of 23rd Street, Antonia makes a wrong turn and heads toward the Malecón.

"Where are we going! We have to go to the airport."

Mari turns around, eyes open very wide: "We're taking you to La Punta. You have to go there."

You can't do this. You can't take my life into your hands. I don't want to see them again—Mother, Father, Mama Angélica waving their handkerchiefs. I'm overcome with the dread that children feel from knowing they can be annihilated.

When we reach the esplanade, Antonia drives onto the curb and parks a few yards from the ocean. The sea spray is so strong that the wipers can't clear the windshield. Mari struggles against the violent wind to hold my door open.

I begin the walk toward the lead-gray ocean. A gust buffets me and sends me spinning toward the seawall; I can hear the waves, hollow and powerful, smashing into the Malecón wall. I hug myself against the cold spray and stumble on toward the sea.

And then, once more, I'm on the stern of the *Guadalupe*, afraid and without defenses. The boat is pulling me away from home. The ocean is yelling: *Jump! JUMP!*

At that instant, an enormous black wave crashes against the Malecón; the spray slaps me and pries open my throat. I hear my own screams:

I didn't die. You see? I'm alive!

I'm spinning in the wind, yelling back at the bully-ocean:

I have not become ashes! I am flesh and blood! You didn't kill me. I came back alive!

※　※　※

The airport official at José Martí Airport leafs through my passport, shakes his head *no* and looks up into my eyes.

No me permite salir.

He's not letting me out.

No voy a ver a mis hijos más nunca.

I'll never see my children again.

No voy a ...

I'll never get home to Buffalo.

Buffalo? Home?

❊   ❊   ❊

As I've cleared customs in Toronto, a familiar voice rings out from the crowds in the terminal.

"Mom! Mom! You're home!"

Scatter My Ashes Over Havana